John Healy was born in Limerick and raised in County Dublin, but moved to the UK in the late fifties. He worked as a TV engineer, then spent twenty-seven years as a London cabbie. John has previously published a children's book, *The Flea and the Cauliflower* (Authorhouse, 2008). He lives in south-west London.

THE TAXI:
I DROVE IT MY WAY

Tales of a London Cabbie

John Adrian Talbot Healy

Book Guild Publishing
Sussex, England

First published in Great Britain in 2013 by
The Book Guild Ltd
The Werks
45 Church Road
Hove, BN3 2BE

Typesetting in Garamond by
Keyboard Services, Luton, Bedfordshire

Printed in Great Britain by
4edge Ltd, Hockley. www.4edge.co.uk

A catalogue record for this book is available from
The British Library

ISBN 978 1 84624 933 4

For Ray

Introduction

Join me on a tour of London – the London I came to know and love over nearly thirty years as a black cab driver. This is a unique insider's view, showing you London life, warts and all; the ups and downs of being a cabbie, including many tales of the famous – and infamous – people I have met over the years.

Everything in this book I believe to be true and has either been told to me or I have read over the many years I've worked in London. However, there may be the odd discrepancy because sometimes facts get distorted as time passes.

Chapter 1

I was a London black cab driver for twenty-seven years. One of my proudest possessions is my certificate from the Public Carriage Office stating that in all that time I never had a single complaint made against me. Mind you, I was wound up by the odd unpleasant customer but then you are bound to encounter a few head-cases over a period of almost three decades.

I sold my cab after my second wife Rosemary developed a dreadful ailment called Motor Neurone disease, which causes the muscles to waste away. She died in 2008 at the age of just 61. I'd always worked days as a cabbie (I hated the abuse and the drunks that you had to deal with at night) and every evening she was there to come home to, with a gentle kiss and a lovely meal on the table. Then suddenly she was gone. My heart was broken.

Black cabs are really called hackney cabs, and according to the London Vintage Taxi Association, the term 'hackney' comes from the Norman French word 'hacquenée', meaning a type of horse suitable for hire. The LVTA says that hackney coaches first appeared in London during the reign of Queen Elizabeth I as a way for the wealthy to recoup some of the enormous expense incurred in keeping coaches by hiring them out to aspiring but less well-heeled members of the gentry. I called mine The Hack, and in it I travelled the length and breadth of London more times than I can count and had more adventures than I can remember. Here I've tried to put down as many recollections as possible by creating a cab journey that meanders around the capital as I recall some of my most exciting – and sometimes distressing – experiences.

1

Before I became a cab driver I was in the television repair business in London. As an electronics engineer, the bulk of my work was in the West End, Belgravia, Kensington, Chelsea and other well-to-do areas. My customers were the rich and famous who lived there, people like Bob Geldof (then with the Boomtown Rats), Eric Clapton and Mick Jagger. At one time, Marianne Faithfull was living in the Jagger household with her young son, so the first stop on our mythical cab tour of London is their house in Cheyne Walk, Chelsea, where I once repaired the colour television. It was early days for colour sets and not many people could afford such expensive televisions at that particular time, so these were rare calls.

The house was very elegant. The hallway had no carpets, just highly polished floorboards, and the carpets were hanging on the walls. Very tasteful and unusual, I remember thinking. Unfortunately, Mick Jagger was out, but Marianne Faithfull escorted me up the stairs to the first floor where I found the defective television. It was evident the fault had been caused by her little boy, who had 'accidentally' poured Ribena into the back of the TV set. It's a good thing it didn't burst into flames and burn their beautiful old house to the ground. Miss Faithfull recorded quite a few records but not many stayed near the top for very long, although I always thought her a pretty good singer. She led a turbulent life with divorce, drugs and illness and I must admit that I had a bit of a crush on this attractive lady, although she was well out of my league.

Chapter 2

Just two or three doors along from where Mick Jagger lived there is a pub called The Kings Head and Eight Bells. In Tudor times they were two different inns, accessible either by road or via the River Thames and frequented by King Henry VIII and his entourage. The Kings Head was the 'posh' pub, used by King Henry, his close relatives, courtiers and ladies-in-waiting from Hampton Court. The Six Bells was for Henry's staff, especially the oarsmen who rowed the mighty royal barge on backbreaking journeys down the Thames from Hampton Court to Westminster. The stopover was a very welcome break, because the rowers would be worn out by the time they reached the inns and in need of food and drink. Eight bells were rung to summon all the staff to help the oarsmen prepare for the next leg of the journey, hence the name of the second inn.

Eventually the two inns were knocked down and a single public house erected on the same site using the name The Kings Head and Eight Bells. This double-named pub is a thriving business to the present day. I was told by a local man it was the only pub in the near vicinity that Mick Jagger was not barred from and that the Rolling Stones used to visit now and then en masse. Who was the more famous, King Henry VIII or Mick Jagger?

Five or six houses in the other direction from the Jagger house there is a blue plaque commemorating the well-known Victorian author George Eliot. As most people know, this writer was not a man as the name suggests but a woman called Mary Anne Evans. The reason she used a male pseudonym was because she wanted her writing to be taken seriously and the Victorians tended to think women wrote only light novels. Her books – including *The Mill on the Floss*, *Middlemarch* and *Silas Marner* – are well-written stories, which I heartily recommend.

Chapter 3

As I continue on my mythical cab journey, we enter Royal Hospital Road. If I turn to the left, we come across Chesil Court where Hayley Mills lived for a while. I have been to the flat on two occasions in a professional capacity but I met this talented young lady long before, when she lived on Richmond Hill in a beautiful old house called The Wick. She was only about nine or ten then and I remember knocking on the door of this fine house, which was answered by a very posh man who I thought was the butler. He looked down his nose at me, and said 'Yeeeeees?', stretching the word out to make it sound long and demeaning, as if I was totally inferior to him. I told him that I was here about the television, and he said in a condescending voice, 'Follow me, sir'.

It was then that Hayley Mills' tiny dog began to harass me, nipping at my ankles. The butler turned on the dog, tapped it with his foot, and muttered, 'F... off'. The dog did exactly that, and we continued our journey to the room where the television was. I noticed a tiny smile creep across his face as he showed me in. Ha, he was human after all! I liked that. Hayley Mills had heard what happened and she laughed her head off.

In 1971, the lovely Hayley married Roy Boulting, one half of the famous Boulting brothers duo, who made films like *Brighton Rock* (1947). The new Mr and Mrs Boulting lived in Lower Belgrave Street but the press upset the couple by writing about the 33-year age difference between them. Hayley Mills starred in films such as *Whistle Down the Wind, Pollyanna* and many more hit movies as well as appearing in the recent hit TV series *Wild at Heart* playing the mother-in-law. What a career to have behind you. If Hayley Mills had married me she would have been called Hayley Healy. Imagine that.

A few years later I had the good fortune to meet Hayley's dad, the even more famous Sir John Mills. I was called to his new flat just off Park Lane when his TV aerial developed a fault. He actually came up on to the flat roof with me and showed great interest in what I was doing. How many film stars would do that? Sir John Mills, who died in 2005 aged 97, was not a very tall man but he had the personality of a giant and I felt honoured to have met such a legend. He starred in such films as *Goodbye, Mr Chips, Ryan's Daughter, Oliver Twist* and *Great Expectations* but actually appeared in more than 120 films over a career spanning seven decades. What a legacy of movies to have left after just one lifetime.

Chapter 4

Just a few houses down from the Boulting brothers' abode was the house of Lord Lucan. He lived there with Lady Lucan, his very petite spouse, and she and their two children were in the drawing room during both my visits. I only saw Lord Lucan the once. As most people know, he is thought to have strangled the nanny, Sandra Rivett. Some say that in the dark basement Lucan mistook her for his wife but I find it very odd that he could have mistaken his tiny wife for a larger woman like Sandra. After Sandra's murder, Lucan vanished into thin air, thus evading a lengthy trial for the alleged murder. Lord Lucan's family name was John Bingham. His friends called him 'Lucky'.

The first time I went to the house as the family's television engineer I met Sandra Rivett and found her a very down-to-earth person. I remember walking up a flight of stairs to where the television set was. At the top of the stairs on the wall there was a large oil painting depicting *The Charge of the Light Brigade*. Lord Lucan's great-great-grandfather was supposed to have been involved in this disastrous folly. The charge was led by Lord Cardigan. Nearly half of the British troops were slaughtered by cannon fire because of this blunder. British troops were fighting the Battle of Balaclava in the Crimean War against the Russians. Whatever were we doing there?

In his famous poem about 'The Charge', Alfred, Lord Tennyson wrote:

> Half a league half a league,
> Half a league onwards,

7

All in the valley of Death
Rode the six hundred.

Across the street in Chester Square lives Margaret Thatcher. She now has a permanent armed police guard outside her house. In the seventies, I remember standing with her in the kitchen of her other house in Flood Street, just off the famous King's Road in Chelsea. It was another television job and she was a Member of Parliament at the time (before she became Prime Minister, of course). Margaret Thatcher was the terror of the 'Gas House', which is what all cabbies affectionately call the House of Commons. One day there will be a blue plaque on the Thatcher house in Flood Street referring to this famous – or infamous – lady. It all depends on one's politics as to which of the two adjectives you choose.

* * *

In 1982, I was called to service the television in the Argentine Embassy. This building is on the corner of Grosvenor Crescent and Belgrave Square. When I had completed the work I was escorted to the front door by a man who was obviously carrying a gun under his coat. (Most internal embassy guards do actually carry arms. It can be a wee bit disturbing, especially if something kicks off.) My armed escort told me in broken English to be careful out there and shut the door very abruptly.

Then it happened, smack in the face: a rotten tomato, lobbed by one of an angry crowd. They were screaming abuse at me, so I took to my heels and ran like the wind, wondering what I had done to deserve such treatment. Only later did I hear on the radio that Argentine troops had invaded the Falklands. The angry, screaming mob were exiled Falklanders that had attacked me, believing I was an Embassy employee.

* * *

Down the road we come to leafy Eaton Square. Many years ago,

8

I remember an old bag lady sat here every day on a bench. I pulled my cab over once and had a chat with her. It was a hot summer's day but she was wearing a fur coat that was fraying at the edges. I found out she had been very posh in her earlier years but she would not tell me what had gone wrong to force her to take to the streets. Someone told me that the singer songwriter Ralph McTell wrote 'Streets Of London' relating to this very person and although there is no proof this is who the song refers to, I would like to think it was my elegant bag lady. I drove away and returned with a Big Mac and a drink, which she very much appreciated.

Chapter 5

Back to Royal Hospital Road. On my right hand side is the Chelsea Physic Garden, known locally as the Secret Garden. It was founded in 1673, for the purpose of training apprentices in identifying plants. Here apothecaries grew all sorts of herbs to try and cure all manner of ailments. I was told they even grew the first strain of cotton for the American southern states. The garden claims to be to be London's oldest botanical garden and is well worth a visit.

Further down the same road we pass Tite Street, home to the famous Irish writer and flamboyant dresser Oscar Wilde. Born in Dublin in 1854 and christened Oscar Fingal O'Flahertie Wills Wilde, he attended Trinity College but was pilloried for being a homosexual, something that would never happen in modern times.

A blue plaque on the Tite Street house commemorates Oscar Wilde's life as author of classics such as *Dorian Gray*, *The Importance of Being Earnest* and *Lady Windermere's Fan*. In 1895 he was imprisoned for having a homosexual affair with a teenage boy – the whole thing was a great scandal in Victorian times – and after a devastating trial, was sentenced to two years' hard labour in Reading prison. He wrote about the experience in *The Ballad of Reading Gaol*. When he was released, the playwright was bankrupt and had lost everything: his wife, his children, his house, the plays, poems and most of the literature that he had written, which had been auctioned off cheaply. Oscar Wilde fled to France and soon after, in 1900, died penniless and was buried in Père Lachaise cemetery, Paris. A few graves along is the resting place of Jim Morrison, American singer/songwriter with The Doors. The band had an unbelievable cult following, and pilgrimages to Morrison's tomb are a regular occurrence. Amazing how famous people still get together, even in death. *The Ballad of Reading Gaol* has well over 100 verses. That is the work of a genius.

A little further along Royal Hospital Road, we find the Army Museum, which contains the skeleton of Napoleon's horse. He must have run out of hay. There is lots of interesting Army memorabilia to be seen at this small museum and it is definitely worth a visit.

Chapter 6

Moving along we come across the Royal Hospital Chelsea, founded by King Charles II in 1682 to look after wounded, homeless and retired old soldiers from all the wars as far back as the late 1600s. King Charles II's father, King Charles I, was beheaded by the Puritan leader Oliver Cromwell and his mob of Roundheads. I like to joke that the first Charles was not a very tall man but when they took his head off he suddenly became even less tall, although I don't think they stood him up to see just how tall he was after decapitation. It's very sad to do that to any human being; after all, he was only doing his job of being King.

I'm told that a few years after Cromwell's death, Loyalists removed the remains from his tomb and mutilated the body. They chopped off his head and displayed it in a public place in order to be mocked.

But enough of the gory stuff. Back we go to the Royal Hospital, a beautiful old building built by Christopher Wren. Today you can observe the retired old soldiers walking around Chelsea in their bright crimson tunics sporting highly polished medals. They are known as the Chelsea Pensioners and display a great sense of pride. It is here in the Royal Hospital grounds the famous Chelsea Flower Show is held every year.

Opposite the Royal Hospital and through Burton's Court we find St Leonard's Terrace. A house with a blue plaque states 'The author of Dracula lived here'. He was an Irish writer called Bram Stoker who got his inspiration from the ruins of a very large medieval abbey in Whitby, North Yorkshire. This abbey was started in 657 AD, and was wrecked by King Henry VIII in 1538. It's an extremely eerie place to be, especially if a mist rolls in from the sea to completely enshroud the skeletal remains of what was once a beautiful building. There are 199 steps to climb to get to this foreboding structure. During World War I a couple of German cruisers took a few pot shots at the remains of this old abbey, bringing down at least two of the flimsy towers.

* * *

Back in London, we are now on the King's Road, heading towards Sloane Square, where we find Royal Avenue. This is the address author Ian Fleming used for James Bond's London flat in his famous spy books.

Here in the King's Road, a very attractive fashion designer called Mary Quant created the mini skirt and hot pants. This world-famous road saw the comings and goings of punks and hippies, and was the 'place to be' in the sixties and seventies. The Stones, the Beatles, Bowie; they were all here and left their mark.

I've seen shops in the King's Road with the strangest names, such as a shoe shop called R. Soles and a Chinese restaurant called Ho Lee Fook. That reminds me, in north London there is a taxidermist shop called 'Get Stuffed'. These are names that one does not easily forget, and that's called good advertising.

* * *

Many a time as I drove my cab along the King's Road, I would observe a man sitting at a table outside a certain restaurant, who, in my opinion, was one of the greatest footballers in the world. He always had a bottle of wine and a full glass on his table, which he would regularly raise to passers-by. Yes, it was the famous George Best. I picked him up one day and took him from one pub to another. I suppose that by doing that I must have played a tiny part in his downfall. George eventually had a liver transplant but even so, the demon drink won the day in the end. I have a great photo that I treasure of him smiling and looking into my cab window. I think it's quite rare because he was nearing the end of his life.

The day Mr Best was in my cab he asked me if I knew any jokes. 'Yes,' I said to him. 'You are from the City of Belfast where the Titanic was built. Well, that ship was not really made in Belfast as you thought. It was rumoured that it was made in the Far East, in Thailand, hence the name "*Thaitanic*". They just spelled it wrong.' (OK, it's a bit weak.)

Anyway, that was only a part of the joke. I went on to say that more people would have been saved if they had listened to the onboard speaker announcement. 'Some people were waiting for the dancing because the ship's Tannoy had said there was a band on ship,' I told him. He did not get the joke straight away, so I said 'Abandon ship!' and then he said, 'Oh, I get it,' and laughed.

Then he told me a joke about the two Northern Irish ducks on a tandem bicycle. The one at the back said, 'Quack' and the one at the front said, 'I can't go no quacker'. I had heard it before but it was nice to have it told in a proper Northern Irish accent. I did laugh.

George Best lived just off the King's Road, near Oakley Street with his lovely [second] wife, Alex, who stood by him for as long as she could. Sadly, he died in 2005. In the same street lived Cynthia Payne, more commonly known as Madam Cyn, whose house of ill repute was some way away in Streatham), and just a few doors along there is a blue plaque to one of the most famous adventurers of all, Robert Falcon Scott of the Antarctic.

* * *

Close by, and spanning the River Thames, is the beautiful and ever-so-flimsy Albert Bridge, built in 1842. This bridge can take most cars but no Rolls Royce or Bentley is allowed across, due to the two-ton weight limit. The Roller and the Bentley each weigh two-and-a-half tons. It must really annoy the owners of these expensive, high-status cars that they cannot legally follow an old banger over the bridge. A black cab is just on the two-ton limit but with four or five large passengers on board it is over, although the boys in blue tend to turn a blind eye.

Some years ago the cab trade fell out with the police and a few cabbies felt the full force of the law. This small disagreement did not last very long as the cab trade and the police tend to work together. There are signs on the bridge requesting troops from the nearby Chelsea Barracks to break their marching step. Can you imagine those troops bringing down this bridge with pure vibration? I am sure it would take at least two or three platoons banging their big heavy boots down on the road surface to do that. The bridge still has the original toll booths, although they are no longer in use.

Chapter 7

Back on my imagined taxi journey I have arrived in Ebury Street, where there is a house with a brown plaque commemorating one of the most famous of all composers and a favourite of mine: Wolfgang Amadeus Mozart. Brown plaques were used exclusively for famous foreign people whereas the blue ones were for well-known British people. The story goes that a member of the Mozart family was seriously ill, so to receive the proper treatment the family came to London and rented the house in Ebury Street. It was here that the young Amadeus wrote his first symphony. Mozart was one of the greatest child prodigies that ever lived and was only 35 when the grim reaper gave him the call. He died a penniless pauper in Vienna in 1791. I wonder what great classical works he would have produced if he had been given just a few more years to live? There is a full-size statue of Mozart at one end of Ebury Street in a small triangular area dividing two roads, lovingly known as Mozart Square. It depicts him as a young boy playing a violin, in dancing mode, dressed in the correct period clothes. It is worth a visit.

They say that a certain composer in Vienna called Antonio Salieri stole or plagiarised some of Mozart's compositions. It was never proved but about twenty years ago sheet music was found in Salieri's loft, which, when played, sounded surprisingly like the work of Wolfgang Amadeus Mozart. I once picked up Simon Callow and asked him was he in the film *Amadeus*. His reply was, 'Perhaps'. Well, I have seen the movie and I know he had a good part, so there was no 'perhaps' about it. How modest can one be?

Continuing our journey, we arrive at swankily expensive and affluent Eaton Square. Barry Gibb of the Bee Gees rented a house here in the late sixties. For a time, I was his private television engineer and I remember him saying he was addicted to his television and could not be without it at any time. That meant he paid me well to be on the phone when he needed me. He was such a handsome devil that I was quite jealous of his looks and his money.

One evening at about nine p.m. the phone rang and my first wife picked up the receiver. After a short time she slammed down the phone, so I asked who the caller was. She said it was some crank caller pretending to be Barry Gibb. Was she surprised when I told her that it really was him! I had forgotten to tell her I was working for him. Luckily he rang back and got a big apology. Then off I went into the night to repair the superstar's television set. He was one of the nicest high profile people I have ever met.

The late Kenny Everett used the Bee Gees' hit song 'Massachusetts' on his crazy funny show. With forty or fifty sets of false teeth on a table, Everett sang 'Mass of Chew Sets' to the same air as the original tune, which was hilarious. I went to Kenny Everett's house once – it was in the Holland Park area. The comedian was sitting on top of a very large colour television set with his usual mad look. 'I expect it's full of gremlins,' he said, and, you know, I really think he meant it. Unfortunately, Kenny Everett died in 1995 at the age of 50. How sad is that.

Chapter 8

The day, the month, the year will never be forgotten. 9/11, 2001. Nothing was ever achieved by that crazy act. We must never forget the thousands of innocent people that were killed and all those loved ones that were left behind to mourn their passing.

That day I knew a Eurostar train was due to arrive from Paris, so I swung my cab into Waterloo Station and joined the other waiting taxis, hoping to get away quickly with a decent fare. It would be my first that day, and my last, because of what was about to happen. This was one day I will never forget.

I drove my cab along the ever-increasing queue of punters, some tired from their journey, some excited and coming home to loved ones, until it was my turn. There they were, four extremely attractive, teenage American girls. They wanted to hear a Cockney accent but were not too disappointed when all I could provide was an Irish brogue. We laughed and joked in the usual way. They told me they were all from New York – from, of all places, Manhattan. They said they had spent some time touring around Europe and London was their last city to visit. The next day they would all fly home from Heathrow. They were very exited about grabbing a tour bus in order to see London, 'the greatest city in the world'.

These lovely New Yorkers were all much larger than me so I did not get in their way as they loaded their own luggage into the baggage compartment. I might have been squashed in the process.

'Where to, ladies?' I enquired. They told me they wanted the Lancaster Hotel in Bayswater, so off we went, manoeuvring with ease around Hyde Park Corner, up Park Lane, around Marble Arch and into Bayswater Road.

It was then that I turned on the radio. I heard the announcer say these two words, 'New York', followed by the word 'Manhattan'. (As I remember this, a tear has fallen on my keyboard and I've had to take a break to dry my eyes so I can continue with this sad tale.)

One of the American girls asked me to turn up the volume and we heard the newsreader say that a plane had crashed into one of the Twin Towers in Manhattan. He said six people had been killed. (How wrong was that man.) He then went on to say in a broken and shaky voice that another plane had crashed into the second tower, and that both buildings were beginning to collapse.

The American girls were weeping and screaming in the back. Tragically, they all had relatives working in the Twin Towers on that fateful day. We were only a few minutes away from the hotel, so I put my foot down to get them to their destination as quickly as possible. The situation was getting out of hand and I couldn't handle it. When we arrived at the Lancaster I ran into the foyer and alerted the head porter, who then emerged with the concierge and another porter. The girls were now guests of the Lancaster Hotel and it was up to the staff to look after them.

I did not take a fare from these distressed girls, it would have been inappropriate. I never saw any of them again but they pop into my mind quite regularly. I hope they all recovered from their awful ordeal in London. As for me, I drove my cab straight home to get over my traumatic day.

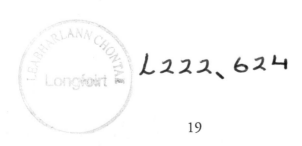

Chapter 9

It was April 1984. I was hailed in the street by a man who wanted me to drive him to an address in St James's Square. When we arrived at the destination, my customer paid the fare and went on his way. I started to leave the Square but my movement was blocked by a chanting crowd of dissident Libyans who were opposed to the dictatorial rule of Colonel Gadaffi. They had gathered just across the road from their embassy and were blocking my exit. A young policewoman cleared a way for me and I was off out into Lower Regent Street with my 'For Hire' light blazing away in order to attract my next customer.

Later I heard on the radio that an automatic gun had sprayed a volley of bullets from the window of the embassy. Around thirteen Libyan protesters were wounded and one policewoman was shot dead. This was the very same lady who had freed me from the Square minutes earlier. I was in the line of fire ten minutes before that murder. It just goes to show that you never know when your time is up.

This poor woman was only doing her job. She was WPC Yvonne Fletcher and thanks to Gadaffi's thugs, she lost her young life. The killer and his henchmen walked free to fly back to Libya. Now, after the 2011 uprising in Libya, the British government might get their hands on the gunman who shot this brave young WPC. Disgraceful behaviour by these people who I call 'thug killer' diplomats.

Chapter 10

I wanted to become a black cab driver for many years. When I was working as a television engineer in the West End, I realised this was a great ambition of mine, so to make my dream come true I went on to do 'The Knowledge'. Apparently, this qualification is equal to a degree. To do The Knowledge entails riding a moped around London Town, the City of London and to a lesser extent the Metropolitan area of Greater London. The latter covers a thirty-five mile radius from Charing Cross.

One must commit to memory all the street names, the history and any landmarks encountered on your daily route. It took me the full four years to obtain my highly-prized green badge but I was in no hurry because I was in full time employment as a TV engineer.

One young man I met on The Knowledge had a photographic memory. He completed the task in just two years and decided to have a celebratory holiday – I think he went to Spain. While he was away he was run over and killed by a taxi cab. What an ironic thing to happen.

* * *

You must wear your badge all the time when driving the cab. If for any reason the driver ever has to appear in court, the law states that the badge must be worn in the dock. Oliver Cromwell was the first person to license the cab trade in 1654. A law dating back 300 years to Cromwell's time stated that a carriage driver had to have a bale of hay in the boot of his vehicle to prevent cruelty to his hungry horse, which would have been out working all day without food. Cromwell's law was certainly good for the poor old nags. The authorities kept that old law on the statute book. It was repealed about ten years ago. The police used that ancient law to stop any cab driver that they wanted to talk to, and would say 'Where's your bale of hay?' Of course, as there was never any hay in modern cabs they could then legitimately search the cab and talk to the suspect driver. What a way to treat cab drivers. We are the Knights of the Road. Sometimes the law really is an ass.

Incidentally, while I was doing the knowledge, I fell off the moped three times, but all I hurt was my pride.

Chapter 11

Our next stop on my mythical tour is The City of London, which is divided from Greater London by an old Roman wall called London Wall. Within it lies the Golden Mile, which is the financial centre where fortunes are made and lost with the press of a button. (The latter seldom happens).

There were many gates into the City of London. They were built by the Romans, but sadly they have all disappeared now, swallowed up by 'progress'. Some bits of London Wall, though, still exist to this day. The Romans built London, constructing a great city in 443 AD that they named Londinium, but they abandoned it in the early fifth century. Apparently Rome was attacked by both Goths and Germanic tribes at the end of the fourth century so the legions all went home to defend their own land, leaving behind them a thriving City that continued to prosper.

Construction workers are still digging up lots of old Roman artefacts including well-preserved tombs and graves. If a new building is to be constructed in the City of London, builders have to allow archaeologists time to start a dig. They get at least one month to unearth the many valuable ancient treasures lying beneath their feet, otherwise all these precious items would be lost forever. The builders are never very happy about this but there is nothing they can do about it. This is the law, although the archaeologists are hard-pressed to find all there is to be found before the cranes and the pile drivers move in.

A team of archaeologists got very excited recently when they unearthed a complete Roman mosaic floor – a rare find, although not as good as when they discovered the remains of a complete

Roman gladiatorial arena within the confines of the beautiful and extremely ornate Guildhall. I believe it was in pretty good condition. One day on my lunch break I parked my cab just outside the hoarding that had been placed around the discovered arena. Peering through the small public viewing window I swear I could almost hear the roar of the tribunes, the centurions and the baying crowd of Romans egging on their champions with their thumbs up or down. One to kill, one to save. How about that! It was a weird and strange experience I had that particular day. Incidentally, a few years ago the Museum of London discovered that the thumbs down sign was not to kill the defeated fighter but to save him, and the thumbs up was permission to kill the unfortunate loser, so films like *Gladiator* and *Spartacus* got it all wrong.

A good friend of mine who was a construction worker in the City told me that about twenty or thirty years ago they dug up a skull on a new Cheapside building site. The police were promptly called and after detailed examination the forensics team proclaimed that the skull was that of a 2,000-year-old Roman, obviously well preserved. Alas, the rest of the bones were never discovered.

I love the name Cheapside. There are others such as Milk Street, Silk Street, Bread Street, Wood Street, Poultry, Cloth Street, New Change, Old Change ... I could fill a whole chapter with these beautiful names but I must press on.

Years ago, a radio programme called The Goon Show indicated that they had just dug up a skull. Harry Secombe said: 'It must be a woman.'

'How do you know?' asked one of the other Goons. 'Well the mouth is still open,' said Harry. I think it's quite funny, but these days it would be viewed as 'not politically correct' by the do-gooders.

Chapter 12

I had just dropped a fare off at the Tower of London and was driving The Hack back along Lower Thames Street. It was then that I noticed a crowd gathering on the corner of Pudding Lane and Monument Street. Curiosity made me swing the cab over to have a nose. There is a plaque on a wall in Pudding Lane stating that the Great Fire of London started here in a baker's shop in 1666. The Monument was built close by to commemorate the Great Fire and celebrate the rebuilding of the City, although this obelisk is not on the exact spot where the fire started.

The assembly of people that day consisted of The Lord Mayor of the City of London, the Worshipful Company of Bakers and lots of dignitaries. The press were also present. I noticed a very small red fire engine dating from the late eighteenth century parked nearby. I asked what was going on and was told that the Worshipful Company of Bakers was here to officially apologise to the Lord Mayor for starting the fire and destroying a major part of London.

The apology was duly accepted. Alas, it was 300 years too late. When asked, 'Why the fire engine?' the Lord Mayor replied, 'We still do not trust you bakers.' There was hilarious laughter all round and it made the evening television news and the next day's newspapers.

A thought that often crosses my mind is whether the Great Fire was deliberately started in order to eliminate all traces of the Great Plague in 1664. At its height this horror claimed up to 7,000 souls per week in London alone, although this doesn't sound a lot compared with the worldwide 'flu pandemic in 1918 which took well over 50 million lives. In London, the Great Plague was caused by rodents that came ashore from foreign trading ships. These rats were infested with fleas which carried the bubonic plague. The Great Fire would have destroyed any remaining rats that carried the diseased fleas but whoever started it did not realise how severe the fire was going to be and it got totally out of control.

The Great Fire destroyed the beautiful old wooden shops and dwelling houses that stretched from one side of the old London Bridge to the other. There are many old paintings in museums depicting this ancient wooden bridge, bustling with everyday life. It's such a shame to have lost such a historic bridge.

In time, a stone bridge was built to replace London Bridge. Years later it was sold to an American businessman. Apparently the Yank thought he was buying Tower Bridge, which is a much more elaborate piece of engineering. The one he purchased was dismantled, stone by stone, and shipped to the Nevada Desert where it was reassembled. It turned out to be a very successful tourist attraction but it wasn't quite what he thought he was getting!

Underneath the present London Bridge in Upper Thames Street there is a church by the name of St Michael Paternoster Royal, associated with the pantomime character Dick Whittington, thought to be Sir Richard Whittington, who lived from 1354 to 1423. I read some years ago that his coffin was moved around a bit when a German doodlebug fell near the church, lost all its markings and is now mixed up with about ten other similar caskets within the church. Sir Richard is believed to have been a poor boy when he first came to London expecting to find the streets paved in gold. Down in spirit, he was leaving the City via Highgate Hill when he is supposed to have heard the sound of Bow Bells telling him to return to London. This he did, and became Lord Mayor of London, not once, not twice but three times. The authorities erected a stone statue of his cat on Highgate Hill, supposedly on the spot where he heard the bells. His story is so loved that is has been immortalised in the pantomime *Dick Whittington*, beloved by children at Christmas time.

Chapter 13

My cab journeys were always leading me back to London Bridge, and a funny thing happened to me once when I was on the taxi rank there. Things were very slow for some reason or other, until the moment my passenger door was suddenly opened by a drunk. He got in by one door and left by the other door almost immediately. He then came to my window and gave me a fifty pence piece, and said 'Thank you very much' before staggering off. The other cabbies and I roared with laughter. That's what too much drink can do to a person. It was the quickest fare that I ever had, I went nowhere and did not even start my engine. But I did get the massive fare of fifty pence.

I felt well pleased when my next fare turned out to be the great actress and now a Member of Parliament, Glenda Jackson. She asked to be taken to the House and I had an awful longing to say 'Your house or mine?' but I resisted.

* * *

Near to London Bridge is Lambeth Palace, a beautiful red brick building, and stuck onto one side is a church called St Mary-at-Lambeth. It is associated with Admiral William Bligh of *The Bounty* (1754 to 1817), who lived round the corner in Lambeth Road and is buried in a large tomb in the rear garden of the church. Some of the Tradescant family, who were botanists, are also buried in this churchyard. They had links with *The Bounty* because the ship sailed on a hunt for breadfruits, but the crew mutinied and that put a temporary halt to their search. There is a large blue plaque on the Lambeth Road house dedicated to Bligh.

The church has had a garden museum for many years, and there is a superb herb garden to the rear. The museum has the actual desk that belonged to Gertrude Jekyll (1843 to 1932), author of fifteen books on Victorian gardening. This lady was extremely famous as a landscape gardener and designed gardens all over the world. There is also a fascinating collection of extremely unusual garden implements dating back hundreds of years and a collection of strange gravestones. One says, 'Here lies Thomas Crisp who died of the thunder and lightning whilst standing at his window.' The church is really worth a visit, at least for an hour or so. All a visitor has to do is to donate a couple of pounds for the upkeep of this rare and unusual building.

Mounted on the outside front wall to the left of the main door of St Mary's is a very large, thick black slate measuring about four feet by three feet. It's an extremely bigoted plaque, even for that time. The bold, heavy, hand-carved wording on this huge slate that dates from the seventeenth century, says that one Bryan Turbervile bequeathed one hundred pounds for the betterment of the local community. It then goes on to say, 'None to be put to chimney-sweepers, watermen or fishermen and no Roman Catholic to enjoy any benefit thereof.' What do you think of that? Is this an early example of discrimination? It's certainly unacceptable prejudice by one person against his fellow man and sadly still exists today.

A short drive down the Lambeth Road we find the famous Lambeth Walk, as immortalised by the song, 'Doing the Lambeth Walk'. It is not what it used to be. Now all you will find are lots of dowdy flats, but if you stop and close your eyes for a moment you can imagine the ghosts of yesteryear, the old music hall soloist giving a rapturous rendering of 'Doing the Lambeth Walk', and the whole audience from the stalls to the balcony singing at the top of their voices. What a vision!

I now drive away from Saint Mary's and cross nearby Lambeth Bridge, turning left along Millbank and heading towards Tate Britain. In the 1800s, Millbank Prison stood on this site. Most of the inmates were awaiting deportation to the colonies – places like Australia. Some had merely stolen a loaf of bread, a silk scarf or committed an even more trivial offence. A large percentage of the deportees did not ever survive the journey as they died from starvation, dysentery, disease, sea sickness, rape, severe beatings or for some other horrible reason.

Across the road and to the right, there is a small pillbox monument to the aforementioned deportees. It is a little larger than the average dustbin. It is made of stone and there is a plaque on the side giving all the information appertaining to these poor souls.

Chapter 14

I was driving along the Embankment once when I was hailed by a well-known millionaire, who asked me to loan him fifty pence to buy a newspaper. When we arrived at his gargantuan property he went into the house to get some cash and when he emerged he said, 'There is your fare, and there is your fifty pence, and this is fifty pence for yourself.' Well! I drove The Hack at breakneck speed to the nearest shop to purchase a lollipop with this huge tip. I would love to say who he was but it would be unfair to his family – they might find out how he was squandering the family fortune. He really was a well-respected character that everybody knows and looked up to and the temptation is killing me but I still cannot reveal his name. He might sue me for my measly few pounds and add it to his millions.

* * *

As I continue on my imaginary tour, I have just dropped off some people at the Temple. This place has some history. Inside, there is the Temple church where you can find nine, full-size stone effigies of the Knights Templar laid out on the floor. It looks very scary.

The church was built by the Knights Templar, who were known as the Crusading Soldier Monks from the order of Saint John in the twelfth century. They were the Crusaders of God and had great influence in the Holy Land and lots of other places such as Malta. Many relics of their escapades can still be found all over the world. In this church they filmed some of the scenes for the movie *The Da Vinci Code*.

Nowadays, the Temple is where all the top lawyers have their Chambers. We are talking money. They make loads of cash out of terrible sadness: divorce, law suits, immigration, human rights, slander etc, and their fees are unreal. A poor labourer earns a fraction of their inflated charges. He would have to work at least a week to earn what they can make in a couple of hours. But if I was a lawyer I probably would do the same as they do.

Chapter 15

We are now leaving the Temple and turning left into Fleet Street. This was the hub of the newspaper world. It's sad that it's all gone now. Most have moved to Wapping and the Docklands area.

At number 186 Fleet Street there was a barbershop on the corner of Bell Yard belonging to the infamous Sweeney Todd. He was credited with over fifty murders, although this number was only an estimate. Todd had a trapdoor under his special barber's chair. He would slit his customers' throats, rob them, and then pull a lever that dropped the client into the basement, where he would carve the best portions of meat from the body. Then his girlfriend, Mrs Lovett, would cook the meat into tasty pies.

This was around the year 1785. The remains of the corpses were hidden under the crypt of the nearby St Dunstan's church but the carved-up bodies started to decay, giving off a foul smell. People complained about the whiff, an investigation was carried out and Todd was apprehended. He was hanged at Tyburn and his body went for medical experiments. So, he too got carved up. However, there is no proof that Todd ever existed and some historians dispute this grisly tale, but where there is smoke, there's fire, I say.

The story of Sweeney Todd first appeared in a magazine known as a 'Penny Dreadful', which was like a comic book for the working man in the 1830s. Charles Dickens wrote a weekly magazine costing one shilling but only the well-off could afford his well-cultured magazine. The 'Penny Dreadful' was for the lower classes. That's all they could afford to pay, one penny. Then came the 'Penny Horrible', the 'Penny Awful', the 'Penny Blood' and various others.

* * *

Driving along Fleet Street we come to Saint Clement Danes church. It is thought to have featured in the old nursery rhyme, 'Oranges and Lemons said the bells of St Clements', although some say that was another church in the City. Anyway, the church in Fleet Street is now called the RAF church. The first Saint Clements church was built in the ninth century, the present one was built by Christopher Wren.

We move along now to the Strand and at some time around the year 2000 I was next on point (at the front of the rank to pick up) at the Savoy Hotel cab rank. The actor Richard Harris lived in these opulent premises and he came to my cab window and asked me to drive him to a specialist wig shop just off Berkeley Square.

He was going to have his head measured for a wig, which he was to wear in a film. For some reason I got the impression that this was the film Harry Potter. I know for sure that he played the part of Professor Albus Dumbledore, head of Hogwarts Academy. During my brief meeting with this extraordinary man he told me he had given up the drink but to me he looked fairly poorly and I could not help feeling that his end was nigh. Harris died soon after my encounter with him and I think the Harry Potter film was the last movie he ever made.

Richard Harris was born in Limerick in Ireland and became a well-established Shakespearean actor who went on to star in *Cromwell*, *The Guns of Navarone* and *Mutiny on the Bounty*. He had so many successful films under his belt. I enquired about the song he once recorded, 'MacArthur Park' and asked him what it was about. It included the words, 'I left the cake out in the rain'. He said, 'I haven't got a clue what that song was about, I just sang it and took the money.' He was quite chatty to me on the cab journey and this might have been because I too was born in the county of Limerick.

* * *

The Savoy Theatre was built in 1889 by impresario Richard D'Oyly. He owned the D'Oyly Carte Company, who performed *The Mikado*, *The Pirates of Penzance* and *HMS Pinafore*, operettas written by Gilbert and Sullivan. Some of the rich and famous who have stayed in the Savoy include Frank Sinatra, Sir Winston Churchill, Charlie Chaplin, Judy Garland, President Harry S Truman, John Wayne, the famous Italian tenor Enrico Caruso, Humphrey Bogart, Elizabeth Taylor, and others too numerous to mention.

Chapter 16

I recall the time I was hailed by a most attractive lady who wanted to go to a place near St Paul's Cathedral. She looked very familiar. As we headed along Fleet Street we got chatting. I showed her some photos of famous people I had previously picked up such as Charlton Heston, Jean Alexander who played Hilda Ogden in *Coronation Street*, Kenneth Williams, Michael Caine and Ken Livingstone. There are really too many to mention. When we got to her destination, she said, 'Go on, take my picture, I am a fairly famous singer'. I did not have my camera that day and I was so annoyed but she just smiled and refused to tell me her name. I'm convinced now that she was Elaine Paige – and I never forgot my camera again.

* * *

There is a fairly large statue of Queen Anne (1665–1714) outside St Paul's Cathedral. The statue is life-size, carved in marble and surrounded by circular railings. Queen Anne had seventeen children and not one of them ever lived beyond the age of twelve. How sad is that, even for a queen.

* * *

There was a time in the late eighties when I had to take a colleague out with me on a television job to repair a colour television for a high-class prostitute in Orange Street, Soho. We rang the bell, which was answered by the maid, who took us into the kitchen and explained that her boss was with a very high profile Government minister in the bedroom. He was having his wicked way and would we mind waiting for a little longer.

When the minister had done the business, the Madam came out of the bedroom wearing only her knickers and bra. She told us that her client did not want to be identified but that the only exit was through the kitchen. The near-naked lady asked us if we would mind holding on to one end of a blanket while she and Romeo held the far end, but they would be on the reverse side. We all held the blanket above our heads and did a little dance. We went to the left, they went to the right. When the half circular dance was completed we found ourselves in the bedroom where the television was. The minister meanwhile was gone in a flash and we did not see his face at all. The harlot gave us £20 each, which was a week's wages at that time. Whatever was the client being charged for his little bit of nookie? My colleague and I left the premises singing 'Blanket Going Round' instead of Blanket on the Ground, the Billie Jo Spears hit.

Chapter 17

I remember picking up a very sweet old lady in the East End once. We got chatting, and during the course of our chat she told me that she was in possession of a rent book for 10 Rillington Place. This was a rare thing indeed. There were about eight women murdered at that premises in the forties and fifties. In 1950, a man called Timothy Evans was wrongly hanged for two of these murders but the real culprit was John Reginald Christie. He murdered Evans's wife and daughter, his own wife and quite a number of innocent girls, plus a number of unwitting prostitutes. He hid the bodies behind wallpaper, in cubby holes, under the floorboards, in the outhouse and in the back garden. He was hanged in 1953 in Pentonville Prison by Albert Pierrepoint, who had also hanged Evans. That rent book must be worth quite a few pounds to the many ghoulish collectors of murder memorabilia.

In 1966, Evans was given a posthumous pardon. They dug him up from his prison grave and he was eventually laid to rest in a proper cemetery. A lot of good that was to him. Rillington Place was eventually pulled down and rebuilt. They changed the name twice because too many people were turning up to see the site where these infamous murders took place and still they kept turning up, so the authorities placed a large gate at the entrance. This gives the present residents much more privacy from the weirdos who gather to stare at nothing.

* * *

I once picked up a young couple from St Pancras Station. They wanted to go to a block of flats in the Oval. Us cabbies had already experienced a bit of trouble with punters from these flats. The man told me that he came from the Caribbean and his girlfriend was English. She was very scantily clad with a giant pair of boobies fully on display. If she looked to the left her boobies swung to the right and vice versa. Anyway, when we arrived at the flats, he opened the passenger door and took to his heels. I wasn't going to give chase so I got out of the cab, went to the already opened door and asked her if she had the metered fare, to which she said no. She then burst into tears, although I think they were crocodile tears. I knew I had lost the fare but I still could not take my eyes away from those non-stop-moving boobies.

At this point a passing police car pulled over. The policemen asked if everything was OK, I told them the situation and one of the cops went to speak to the girl. He went back to the squad car with a big smile on his face.

Then all four of the policemen took it in turns to talk to the girl. It was really only to have a stare at this well-stacked, 'abandoned' female. They wanted to take her down to the police station but I said no. I did not want the bother of having to be a witness in court, not to mention all that paperwork, so I told her to f... off.

I thought that I was reasonably polite. I knew this Caribbean scrote was probably waiting for her around the corner and they would walk away laughing and I would have to take the loss. It was only about £15 or so and we always had cash put by for such occurrences.

Then there was a time when a call girl changed her knickers and bra in the back of my cab while on her way to a customer who had phoned her from the Hilton Hotel. She did not mind me having the odd peek in the rear mirror. The trouble was, she threw all her old underclothes out of the window, but she smiled in such a sexy way and she was a good tipper. The temptation for me to be her next customer was unbelievable but I was a happy and contented husband and only entertained those naughty thoughts for a little while. The thing that worried me most was if the knickers and brassiere had flown out of my cab window and wrapped themselves around a pedestrian's face. What if they had taken my cab number and reported me to the police? My licence could have been suspended.

* * *

As a television engineer I was once called to Ten Downing Street. In the early eighties there were no high iron gates or the extreme security we have today. I parked my company car immediately outside the main door, rang the bell of that famous black door and was admitted straightaway. They did not even open my special television service bag. It was a strange feeling as I found myself in a vast hallway. Suddenly I was surrounded by a lot of burly policemen. They had recognised my Irish accent and as the IRA were doing a lot of bombing at that time I was an immediate suspect. It was a wee bit scary and there were guns about, but all my paperwork was in order.

Not many people can say that they have ever been through that glossy black door. The television was in the top floor flat and belonged to the main Downing Street caretaker who lived there and had seen lots and lots of prime ministers come and go over the past forty or so years. Ted Heath had just become the new prime minister but he never watched television and did not even possess one.

The caretaker's TV was not repairable so I took the set out of the building and placed it on the pavement next to my car, just as a couple of American tourists were passing. They asked me if that was the prime minister's television, and I am afraid I said yes. They then asked if they could photograph it so again I said yes and placed my left foot on the set. They then photographed my left foot plus the telly, and must have told all their friends in America that this was Ted Heath's set. I must say, I did feel a bit of a rogue after telling those little white lies.

Chapter 18

I once had to deliver a very large bunch of flowers to Betty Boothroyd, who was the then speaker of the House of Commons. She had a private flat in the inner courtyard of the Commons and was a very feared and powerful woman in Parliament. Her flat was close to St Stephen's Tower, which houses Big Ben. Tourists go home and tell their friends that they have seen Big Ben but that's not true, they can only hear Big Ben. It's a giant bell that weighs nearly fourteen tonnes, which is about equal to seven London taxis hanging from a crane. That's some weight for a bell. By the way, the total length of the minute hands on the clock face measure a massive fourteen feet.

When I had delivered the flowers and was just about to get into my cab, the bell struck the hour. I was directly underneath the tower. My hearing is very sensitive and I could not believe the booming sound that echoed through my head. I have never heard anything like it and do not want to experience anything like it ever again. Imagine if you were actually in the bell tower of St Stephen's when the clock struck the hour of twelve?

There is a pretty big clock on Shell Mex House in the Strand, facing the Thames. This timepiece is lovingly known in the cab trade as Big Bengie. There used to be a fifteen-foot replica of Big Ben that stood outside Victoria Station called Little Ben. So we have Big Ben, Little Ben and Big Bengie. That is the end of the clock stories, and no, I am not winding you up.

When I was leaving the Commons I was asked to wait at the Members' door. There was a fare emerging. Well, when I saw the ever-so-large Member of Parliament for Rochdale, Sir Cyril Smith, heading towards my cab, I nearly died. He was enormous. When he started to enter the offside passenger door the cab groaned under the weight and leaned to the left. These London cabs are extremely sturdy, so it wasn't a problem and off we went to St Pancras Station.

I have actually had worse than that in my cab in the form of two giant Sumo wrestlers. They had to get in on opposite doors at the same time in order not to create an imbalance and tip the cab over! They were very good tippers but they had to remove each other's wallets from their back pockets because the fat was everywhere and their arms were a wee bit short.

Chapter 19

I was on the rank at the King's Cross Hilton one day when the lady concierge came to my cab window and asked if I could take a guest to St Mary's Hospital, Paddington, and drop her off at the Accident & Emergency department. This foreign lady was very ill and deteriorating rapidly, she said. The hotel staff had tried in vain to get an ambulance but there was nothing available.

The concierge and a porter assisted a frail woman of about forty into my cab. When she was firmly installed behind me, I could see the anguish in her eyes and the fear we might not make it in time. The porter said he thought she'd had a heart attack. I asked the concierge to ring the A&E department to alert them that we were on our way and put my foot down, but when we reached Euston Road we hit the traffic. Luckily I saw a police car and sounded my very loud hooter, to which they responded. I informed them of the situation and they immediately said, 'Follow us'. Well! They cleared a way through that traffic like Moses parting the waters, with me hot on their tail. I was breaking the speed limit with the blessing of the law.

We sped along the Euston Road, into the Marylebone Road and were there in no time at all. As we pulled up at A&E, I could see a whole team of nurses, doctors, porters and a host of medical equipment at the ready. The doctors were in the back of my cab straightaway. I could not even open my door to get out of the cab with all the milling medics.

They quickly fitted an oxygen mask to my fare's face to help her breathe, and started doing some tests. I could not believe what happened next: the patient would not leave my cab until she had paid the fare. I insisted she should not bother as there were more pressing things to get on with such as her immediate treatment, but she would not budge. This lovely lady handed her handbag to one of the doctors and made him take the fare from her purse and pay me. The meter was not even on but she gave me £20. If I did not take the cash, there would be no moving her into the hospital, so I took the fare.

Straightaway the doctors had her in a special wheelchair and wheeled her straight into A&E. I never saw this lady again and do not know how she got on. Did she survive the heart attack? I sincerely hope so, but I will never know unless she reads this book and gets in contact.

Chapter 20

I once had a fare to Lord's Cricket Ground. The passenger told me he was on the committee at Lord's. As we drove through Dorset Square I pointed to a green hut that looked like a garden shed. There are two plaques on the door and I asked him if he knew what it was all about. I was surprised when he said no. The plaques on the door state that this was the original home of Lord's Cricket Ground. Thomas Lord was the head groundsman and as the fans grew in number they had to move to their present home in St John's Wood. Thomas Lord took all the topsoil from this tiny square to the new site. He had nursed this high quality loam for years and he would not leave it behind. The new cricket club grew in popularity and became one of the most famous in the world. They called it Lord's, after him. What a great honour for the groundsman to have the new cricket club named in his memory, not that my fare knew that. How can you be a bigwig at Lord's and not know its history?

* * *

Leaving Dorset Square on my re-created cab journey, I pass Chagford Street, where there is a blue plaque on a garage door. This sign is not to any man or woman but to a car. It reads: 'Out of these garage doors, which are the original, rolled the very first Bentley in 1919.' This was the prototype and its number plate reads NUMBER ONE. This was the birthplace of the Bentley car. How about that for useless information!

* * *

44

If I turn right and drive down from the top of Baker Street, I pass Number 221b on the right hand side. This is the legendary address of Sherlock Holmes. It is now a museum visited by people from all over the world, especially America. The staff regularly get mail addressed to Sherlock or even to Dr Watson. Some of these letters ask the famous sleuth to solve the odd mystery, even though he never existed, but then some people are dreamers and there is no harm in that. Sherlock Holmes' study has been re-created from the writings of the books to a high degree of accuracy. It all looks impressively authentic with Holmes' deerstalker hat and violin on display for all to see. And there is always a policeman dressed in nineteenth century uniform standing outside during opening hours.

Chapter 21

Across Baker Street from the Sherlock Holmes museum is the lost property office. At the time of writing this book there is a small exhibition of unusual things that were lost long ago displayed in the window. One particular piece of lost property that took my interest was an item that was left on a number 23 bus in 1934: an old, coal-heated smoothing iron. How can one lose such a thing and whatever was it doing on the bus? It was never claimed and I'm sure it never will be.

Crossing the Marylebone Road and continuing down Baker Street we come across a blue plaque high up on a second floor flat. It is dedicated to the talented Beatle John Lennon who lived here for a period of time. It's a shame he ever left this flat to go to America just to get shot by a Yankee nutcase. John Lennon had a lot of lovely tunes still to write but his young life was taken away for no reason at all. Who knows what great masterpieces were lurking in the back of his mind? They were all snuffed out like the flame of a dying candle. Lennon and McCartney's music will live on forever.

As I continue down Baker Street I cross George Street, where I remember being called out to a television repair in the eighties. I recall that I was kneeling behind the large colour set and when I got it going, I stood up – only to see the customer standing there with his trousers dropped, enjoying himself with one hand. Now, that is a horrible sight for a working man. I looked at the screen and realised he must have been watching a blue movie the previous day when the television broke down. When I got it going the video had started automatically, the customer had got excited and started doing what he was doing, forgetting I was still behind the television. I ran for the door and legged it like a gazelle. I am glad to say that the company I worked for terminated his contract immediately. I can do without people like that.

* * *

We are now passing Selfridges where I was once hailed by the lady who starred as M in some of the James Bond films, Dame Judi Dench. She wanted to go to Sotheby's in Bond Street. Actually there is no such place as Bond Street but there is New Bond Street and Old Bond Street. Anyway, as the cab was going down Brook Street I pointed out two joined-up houses with a plaque on the outside wall of each building. One said Jimi Hendrix had lived there, the other said George Frederick Handel once lived there (that's the guy who wrote *Messiah* and the famous *Water Music*). Miss Dench said that she had never noticed these plaques before, and was quite impressed.

She then said, 'I bet Handel is turning over in his grave at the difference in their music,' so I thought I would try one of my cornball jokes on her. I asked her if she knew what was written on Fredrick Handel's coffin. She said no, and I said, 'Handle with care'. She thought it was a fairly good joke, had a little giggle and said she would use it in the future.

I dropped this very pleasant lady outside Sotheby's and lingered a while to see her disappear through the auction house doors. In my mind, I jokingly wondered how much she was sold for, and I laughed at my daft thought. But I am sure that she is priceless. It was lovely to have actually met one of the fictional Bond crowd in real life.

Outside Sotheby's there is a small Egyptian statue over the door of a lion-shaped goddess called Sekhmet, the warrior goddess and goddess of healing for Upper Egypt. The black basalt statue is about three feet tall and is the oldest outside statue in London, dating to around 1320 BC. It has been Sotheby's muse since the

1880s, when it was sold at auction for £40 but was never collected. I would like to think that the buyer is now in heaven, looking down at the statue, and wondering if it will ever be delivered up to the Pearly Gates by DHL. After all, they say they will deliver anything anywhere.

* * *

Another extremely old statue in London is Cleopatra's Needle on the Embankment. It dates back to around 1460 BC and is covered with ancient Egyptian hieroglyphs. When the Needle was being installed on the Embankment in 1878, they sealed a time capsule inside its base. There are copies of daily newspapers, some cigars, a packet of hair pins, a railway ticket, cigarettes, photographs of some of the most beautiful women of the time, a full set of coins of the realm and various other artefacts.

This giant obelisk was discovered deep in the sands of Alexandria, where it had lain for nearly 2,000 years. In 1877, it was on its way to England by barge but the tow ropes broke in a storm off the Bay of Biscay. Six men lost their lives trying to secure the tow ropes and their names are written at the base of the obelisk. There are actually three of these giant monuments, one in London, one in Paris, and the third in Central Park, New York.

* * *

On the other side of New Bond Street there is a blue plaque dedicated to the memory of the famous Admiral Horatio Nelson, one of England's greatest heroes. He lost the sight in his right eye in 1794, but not in a battle as some people think. Later on in his adventurous life he was on board the Victory when he was shot dead by a sniper on a French vessel. This was the Battle of Trafalgar, in which he won the day. The crew placed his body in a barrel of brandy to preserve it so he could be returned to England intact. Apparently, some sailors did not know that he was in the brandy barrel, tapped off a couple tots and consumed them. They must have felt sick when they were told that Nelson was in the barrel. He was laid to rest in a large tomb in St Paul's Cathedral.

* * *

We move along now to Bruton Street where we find another plaque on a modern building stating that the present Queen Elizabeth was born in a house on this site. She lived here with her mum, Elizabeth, and her father George. The house has long since been demolished.

When Edward VIII abdicated over his love for an American divorcee called Mrs Simpson, his brother George became king and Elizabeth became queen. They then moved to Buckingham Palace. George died when the young Elizabeth was abroad, and was quickly recalled for the state funeral. She was then crowned Queen Elizabeth and her mother became affectionately known as the Queen Mother.

* * *

Just around the corner from Berkeley Square in Charles Street there is a pub with a very long name: 'I Am The Only Running Footman'. Apparently the original footmen were employed to run in front of their bosses' carriages and clear the way with a big stick through the milling crowds of peasants. (We are talking about between the sixteenth and seventeenth century when life was cheap.) Years later, footmen became the understudies to the butler in wealthy houses, chosen for their charm, height, muscular appearance, good looks and mainly their trustworthy character.

Chapter 22

I was hailed one day in Park Lane by a very distressed lady who said she had just been dumped by her lover of ten years. I hate having to deal with these emotional issues. She was crying all the way to her home in Pimlico and told me she was going to end it all the moment she got indoors. When we arrived I got out of the cab and sat down beside her in the passenger seat. It took nearly half an hour to calm her down and get a promise from her that she would do nothing rash. I had forgotten to turn the meter off and all the time I was consoling the passenger it was running, but I had to write off the £30. Anyway, I was well pleased when I saw the same lady a few days later, smiling and looking very happy. Maybe I missed my vocation and should have been a psychiatrist instead of a cabbie. I really felt good and I was proud to think I may have contributed to the saving of one single life ... or was she pulling the wool over my eyes for a free taxi ride?

A gent hailed me once and said to me, 'Selfridges', to which I replied, 'No, I just drive the cab'. Get it? Sell Fridges ... I don't think he got my trivial little joke so I just took him to where he wanted to go in total silence. Yes, you guessed it, again no tip.

A long time ago, I thought that I had the President of France in the back of my cab. He kept saying, 'Meter on, meter on'. It's only a joke. For younger readers, Francois Mitterrand was once the French president, it's actually pronounced 'Meter on'.

* * *

50

As a television technician, I was a private engineer to the fabulous Hattie Jacques (1922–1980), who lived in a first floor flat in Eardley Crescent, just a few yards away from the Earls Court exhibition halls. She was a giant lady but with a voice as gentle as an angel and was best known for her matron scenes in the *Carry On* movies. Once she rang me at home and asked if I could pick her up and take her to her ex-husband's house. He was John Le Mesurier, and his girlfriend's television had gone wrong. Well, when she sat in my car the vehicle leaned away to the left. Her chest actually touched the dashboard.

I have never met anybody with such a radiant personality. She told me that she had had a major tragedy in her immediate family but I do not want to write about that particular event as it might be hurtful to somebody. They placed a plaque outside her house next to one of the windows. Whenever I drive past Eardley Crescent, I look up and give a sad little sigh to the memory of one of my better customers. John Le Mesurier got me all the signatures of the *Dad's Army* cast but unfortunately I lost the lot. I think my kids may have swapped them for comic books. What a great loss.

Carrying on with my tour, I now leave Eardley Crescent and turn left into Warwick Road, then right into Cromwell Road. On the left is Logan Place where the star of one of the most famous of all pop groups lived: Queen. The star was Freddie Mercury and even today there are lots of flowers left outside his door by adoring fans. It seems he will never be forgotten.

I continue my imaginary journey along Cromwell Road to another blue plaque commemorating a very famous English man, Alfred Hitchcock. He went to America and made such Hollywood greats as *The Birds, Rear Window* and *Psycho*. A master of suspense, he always appeared in a cameo roll in every one of his films, lurking in the background.

Chapter 23

I have now moved up to Kensington High Street and I'm passing Kensington Palace, where Princess Diana lived. I will never forget the day she died, the whole area was covered in flowers, soft toys, framed photos and a multitude of affectionate memorabilia. It was a sea of tributes spread over so much ground.

A few years previously I remember driving my cab down Sloane Street when Diana tried to cross the road to reach her car, which was driven by her bodyguard. I did not brake in time and she smiled at me and walked behind my cab to cross the road. I guess that was the day that I blew my chances of a knighthood. I was surprised at the negligence of her bodyguard. He had left her alone in a street in London on the other side of that road. How bad is that?

I remember the Princess was a regular user of a gym in Townmead Road, SW6, called The Harbour Club. I took many a posh customer there. The paparazzi drove poor old Diana mad by standing on tall stepladders and peering over the ten-foot wall of the gym. They would wait for hours to get a valuable photograph and were there most mornings as I passed by in my cab.

When Prince Charles was courting the young Diana, she lived in a large block of upmarket flats in Old Brompton Road, near Earls Court. If they ever erect a blue plaque to the Princess outside her old apartment that flat will fetch a fortune.

* * *

I now turn right into Queensgate and on the right hand side is a house with the number two on the door. There is a large blue

52

plaque here to the famous comedian Benny Hill. This was his town house. Every time I had a few Americans in the cab, and pointed out this house, they always shouted, 'Stop the cab'. My passengers would all pile out and take photos. The same applied to most tourists, particularly the Japanese. Everybody loved Benny Hill, and any time I pointed out something interesting resulted in a larger tip.

If I continue on down Queensgate we come across the Onslow Court Hotel. This hotel featured prominently in the escapades of the mass murderer John George Haigh, the Acid Bath murderer. He was a long-time guest here and charmed elderly widows and spinsters to invest in his manufacturing outlet in Croydon. The business did not even exist but he did have a run-down premises in Croydon. He would lure these vulnerable people to his so-called factory and shoot them dead.

He then placed their bodies in a vat of acid. After a week or so he would pour away the remaining sludge on the ground at the rear of the factory. Haigh made the classic mistake of thinking that acid would dissolve everything and that if there was no body, there could be no charge. He was so wrong. One of the top police pathologists, Dr Keith Simpson, discovered plastic false teeth, gallstones and fingernails in the sludge, and this was his downfall. John George Haigh was hanged in Wandsworth Prison in 1949. Apparently the hangman could not keep his trap shut...

That hangman was (again) Albert Pierrepoint. He had once executed twenty to thirty women in one day after the Nuremberg trials in Germany, all Nazis that had been convicted of horrendous crimes in the death camps. I read somewhere that he said he always felt a little sorry for those he was about to drop but this was the only time that the same feeling never came over him and he was glad to rid the world of these cruel women. Pierrepoint's book *Executioner Pierrepoint: An Autobiography* is a really great read.

Dr Keith Simpson became a leading pathologist and went on to solve many a high profile crime, but the man who was his tutor was once the most respected pathologist in England. His name was Sir Bernard Spillsbury and he was a leading figure in the Dr Crippen case. This man was so famous in those days that they even erected a blue plaque in his honour. Sadly, Spillsbury committed suicide and one of his pupils carried out the autopsy on him. That pupil was Keith Simpson. How uncanny is that, to open up your own mentor and have a look inside.

Speaking of Dr Crippen, he murdered his allegedly promiscuous wife Cora and fled back home to America with a woman dressed as a boy called Ethel Le Neve. Half way to America the captain of the ship recognised Dr Hawley Harvey Crippen, and used the newly developed ship's wireless system to alert the London police. Two detectives were dispatched to the States on a fast steamer and were waiting for the pair of runaways when the ship docked.

Crippen and Le Neve were returned to London for trial and Crippen was hanged at Pentonville Prison in 1910. This was the first time that wireless was used to capture wanted fugitives. I have always felt a little sorry for this small meek man who fell in love with another woman. His wife treated him with the utmost contempt. Fairly new evidence has come to light recently and it seems that the body found at the Crippen home was not that of his wife. Today, there are a few relatives who want the case re-opened. I wonder what they would find with today's high quality forensics?

The Crippen house has long since been torn down and a block of flats built in its place. People who take London murder tours end up being driven past this block of apartments but there really is nothing to see.

Chapter 24

I once picked up a couple of Americans from the Cumberland Hotel at Marble Arch. They had their thirteen-year-old son with them and said that they wanted Paddington Station. When we got there they asked for platform nine-and-three-quarters. Well! I nearly fell out of my cab door. First of all, it was the wrong station – it should have been King's Cross – and secondly they were on about Harry Potter, who never existed. They must have seen the film and really believed in his existence. If he was a real character and grew a beard, would they have called him 'Hairy Potter'? Ha ha. Anyway, I told them it was only fantasy.

In King's Cross Station there is a baggage trolley that disappears half way through one of the platform walls, in line with scenes from the films when Harry and his friends are returning to school. I could plainly see that these people were somewhat disappointed and they said that they wanted to go back to the hotel. So as I was doing my U-turn near to St Mary's Hospital, I showed them a plaque on the wall stating that Alexander Fleming made the great discovery of penicillin in the room on the second floor in 1928. Some culture dishes had been on the table over the weekend and when they came back days later there were strange growths on the plates. It all took off from then and was perfected in 1940, with help from the Yanks, and was a real lifesaver in the last war. My Americans were so grumpy, they even claimed that it was them that discovered the penicillin but without Fleming they would have gotten nowhere. I was glad to see them disappear through the hotel doors, and yes, you guessed it, no tip again. But I still like most Americans.

55

* * *

Just around the corner is Marble Arch. These were the original gates to Buckingham Palace and there are actually a couple of rooms inside the Arch that were used for the comfort of the gate men. As landau carriages and larger coaches had difficulty getting through the gates the arch was dismantled and moved to its present site at the top of Park Lane. I believe it was replaced with the beautiful marble Queen Victoria Memorial. This enormous work of art was taken from the design of the wedding cake of Albert and Victoria and is known to all London cabbies as the QVM, or more affectionately as 'The Wedding Cake'.

* * *

If you walk down the Mall, have a look at each lamp post and note the large ship at the top of every street light in the form of galleons. They say that Lord Nelson is supposed to be looking at his ships in the Mall from his column in nearby Trafalgar Square but I think the Admiral is actually looking towards Whitehall. Anyway, Nelson never had any galleons.

We now drive around Marble Arch where we can find a small circular plaque on a triangular pavement. It states it is 'The site of Tyburn Tree'. This is the spot where public executions were carried out during and after the fifteenth century. The first gallows was set up in Tyburn in 1571. By the eighteenth century a new type of gibbet was used for public hangings called the Tyburn Tree, where they could hang at least three people at the same time. Executions at Tyburn were like a big festival. There was food, trinket stalls, musicians, street acrobats, whores and a whole host of entertainment going on whilst awaiting the arrival of the condemned criminals from Newgate Prison, which was about four miles away.

The procession would leave in a prison cart full of condemned criminals, drawn by a couple of horses. The group would stop at an inn for refreshments such as beer swigging. This was in the St Giles area. The gaolers would have 'one for the road' but the condemned were not allowed any drink as they were 'on the wagon'. This is supposed to be where the sayings came from.

When Newgate Prison was knocked down, the Old Bailey was built on the site. There is a pub nearby, The Viaduct Tavern, at the eastern end of Holborn Viaduct, where one can still find remnants of this feared prison. All you have to do is to ask the landlord and he will take you down into the basement, and then down a little deeper. Here he will show you the remnants of five of the original cells of this old gaol. It may be that the condemned men and women were glad of death just to get away from their sadistic, Quasimodo-type gaolers who would beat, rape and rob these poor unfortunates inmates. Can you imagine the hygiene, it must have been hell on earth.

Chapter 25

Nearby is West Smithfield, where there is a beautifully designed marble memorial telling the reader that this is the very spot where they executed Sir William Wallace, the Scottish Knight who became a rebel and eventually a martyr. A movie was made about his exploits called *Braveheart*, starring Mel Gibson. The executioner only partially hung him, then drew out his intestines while still alive and finally quartered this poor devil. They sent the arms and the legs to the four corners of England and his head was stuck on a spike on London Bridge. He most certainly went to pieces. How evil is that?

Every time Scotland is playing football at Wembley you will find a crowd of Scottish fans, in their kilts with all the Scottish regalia, laying flowers and standing around this large plaque in silence. I think this is what one calls true patriotism. Wallace died in 1305, the execution ordered by King Edward I, whose nickname was Longshanks. He hated the Scots, the Welsh and the Irish. I think they are all lovely people and they all love the English. Well, most of them do.

Nearby one can find St Bartholomew's Hospital – Barts for short. Founded by King Henry I, and reformed by Henry VIII in 1546, there has been a hospital here for 900 years. Henry was better known for knocking down churches and chopping off the heads of his many wives and his enemies, so reforming Barts was one of the few good things he did in his turbulent life. There is a statue of him above the main entrance.

* * *

Not far away is St Sepulchre's church, founded in the twelfth century and rebuilt in the fifteenth. There is a large hand bell in a glass case in the church that was always rung just before an impending execution. The cemetery of this church has the only watch-house left intact in London. Erected in the eighteenth century and rebuilt after the last world war, the bereaved had to pay men to watch the grave of a deceased family member to protect the corpse from grave robbers. After a month had elapsed the body was not in a fit state to be sold for dissection so there was no longer any need to keep watch. These body snatchers would dig up a new grave and sell the corpse to Barts. The hospital always needed fresh cadavers to teach anatomy and surgical skills. There was even a price list. The fresh body of a young Jewish girl, for instance, would fetch the highest price. Young corpses were in high demand and sometimes the watchmen had two employers: the bereaved family who would pay them to watch, and the grave robbers who would pay them to turn a blind eye. They could not lose.

The most famous of all grave robbers were Burke and Hare, two nineteenth-century grave robbers who found a lucrative business providing cadavers for an Edinburgh medical school. Hare betrayed the other for immunity from execution and Burke was hanged in 1830. After they were apprehended they told the authorities that they actually only robbed one or two graves but had then started murdering to order, which was apparently less strenuous work. They always had a full order book for bodies. These two murdering scallywags killed sixteen innocent people, including two cripples, some whores and drunks. They never left a mark on their bodies that may have been connected to a murder. A movie was made about the Edinburgh body snatchers showing them digging up a grave in some fog-locked cemetery. It certainly painted a gruesome picture.

The robbing of graves was punishable by death at the end of a rope and I do believe a price list still exists to this day in some museum or other. It may be in the London Hospital museum, where the skeleton of Joseph Merrick the Elephant Man is kept. I remember seeing the list on some television documentary a very long time ago. It's hard to imagine a price list for the deceased.

Top left: The late Kenneth Williams.
Top right: The great George Best.
Bottom: Frank Carson, "It's the way I tell 'em".

Top: The site where WPC Yvonne Fletcher was murdered.
Below: George Melly, flamboyant jazz man.

Top: The black spot on the number 2 marks the time when the axe fell on King Charles I.

Below: The smallest police station in the UK.

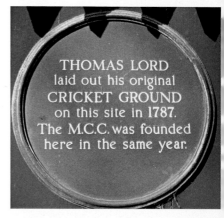

Top: Monument to animals in war.

Middle left: Lost property: a steaming iron left on a bus in 1934.

Middle right: Plaque to Thomas Lord, Lord's cricket groundsman.

Bottom: The Sherlock Holmes Museum, 221b Baker Street.

Top left: Jean Alexander, who played Hilda Ogden in *Coronation Street*.
Top right: Ken Livingstone, former Lord Mayor of London.
Middle: The famous Charlton Heston and wife at my cab window.
Bottom: Richard Harris, actor.

Top: Site of the Tyburn hanging tree.
Below: The very dead Jeremy Bentham.

Top: My taxi being overtaken by a motorised bed.
Below: The Porters Rest, Picadilly.

Left: The Author, age eleven.

Below: The Author with his bundle of twins, a long time ago.

Chapter 26

Referring to the Old Bailey, I recently joined an Over Fifty's club in Wandsworth, south west London, and the organisers arranged for an evening's visit to this most famous courthouse. Twenty or thirty of us all met up at St Paul's tube station. When we arrived at a side door of the Bailey, we were greeted by a man who looked and dressed like a judge. He did these tours because he took great pleasure in showing visitors around. We were taken straight to the number one court and divided into groups.

Some were put in the jury box, others were installed in the witness box and the rest were sent to the public gallery. But one lady and I were ordered into the dock and told to be quiet. Apparently, we were the Accused.

The scene was set. A little mock trial took place in order to give us a feeling of how the courts work. What an experience, none of the public are usually allowed in this dock. It felt like the real thing. 'My female friend and I know that we are innocent, M'lud.'

It was here that the infamous were tried for horrendous crimes, such as the Yorkshire Ripper, Lord Ha Ha, The Kray twins, Dr Crippen, Dr Harold Shipman, and far too many other criminals to be included in these short chapters. To think I have stood in the exact spot where those scoundrels stood makes me shudder.

I remember in the old black and white crime movies the judge would wear the black piece of cloth on his head, sentence the villain to death and then say, 'Take him down'. I now know what he meant. I was able to look down the dingy, dimly lit stairs that he was referring to, a white tiled stairway leading to the temporary holding cells where the accused was held. Later they took us all down for a little tour of this grim and foreboding place.

When the tour was over, most of us went to the pub across the road. It's the one that I mentioned earlier, The Viaduct Tavern, which has access to what is left of Newgate Prison. What a great night! Only the chosen few can experience entry to the number one dock of the Old Bailey, unless you commit murder most foul.

* * *

Quite a few years ago I was driving four foreign people to Lincoln's Inn Fields in London. As we were very near to Portugal Street I thought they might like to see the Old Curiosity Shop that was immortalised by Charles Dickens in his novel of the same name. This sixteenth-century shop looks so old that one would think that it was just about to fall down. It survived the Great Fire and the German bombings. A friend of mine whose father owned the shop once took me into it and let me have a look upstairs. Whilst inside, I was mentally transported back to the Dickensian era. Talk about ramshackle. It had old crooked wooden beams with lath and horsehair plaster. I could see that it was really authentic but my passengers were not the slightest bit interested in this old shop. To tell you the truth I don't even think they had even heard of Charles Dickens. Again no tip – but that never did worry me.

Charles John Huffam Dickens (1812–1870) had a house nearby, 48 Doughty Street, which is now a museum. It should be number one on every tourist's list. If you put your mind to it you can feel the presence of this great writer as you enter the museum. This was the place where he wrote *Nicholas Nickleby* and *Oliver Twist*, in around 1838. You can almost hear the word 'more' echoing around the old living room.

Dickens was a great reformer in his day. Two of his daughters were born in that house, and his sister died in the same building.

In total, he fathered ten children, so he can't always have been writing! He wrote *David Copperfield* at another house in Broadstairs, Kent, which was turned into a really good Dickens museum but is now in private ownership.

When Dickens was twelve, his father was imprisoned in the notorious Marshalsea debtors' prison in Southwark. He was totally insolvent. The family were left without cash and the young Charles had to take a job working at a boot blacking factory.

I believe some relatives are still around to this day, because they all assembled recently at Westminster Abbey to commemorate his 200th anniversary and Prince Charles laid a wreath on his tomb. He is buried in one of the world's most prestigious places, Poets' Corner, in the splendour of Westminster Abbey.

Is it not ironic that I am writing about Dickens, and in a previous chapter I wrote about John Mills who, as a young man, played Pip in the Dickens novel, *Great Expectations?* The film of the book was made in 1946 and also starred a teenage Jean Simmons. Charles Dickens died before he finished his very last book, *The Mystery of Edwin Drood.* What a weird name.

Chapter 27

I was on the taxi rank at the Churchill Hotel when out came Jean Alexander, who used to play Hilda Ogden in *Coronation Street*. She wanted to go to Euston Station and on the way we had a little chat about Corrie. Poor old Stanley had shuffled off this mortal coil and left dear old Hilda all alone. (Of course, this was all just a story written for the soap opera.) I asked her about those famous flying ducks on the wall of her living room wall, and she said it would have been nice if they'd all flown off out of the window as they drove her mad. I asked her could I take a photo of a legend. 'No,' she replied, 'but you can take one of me.' I thought the remark was quite witty. Then she said, 'Wait until I comb my hair'. So the hair combing took place and I got a lovely picture of the famous Hilda Ogden in my taxi.

* * *

I have a great photograph of the movie star Charlton Heston, who starred in movies like *Ben Hur*, *The Ten Commandments* and *Planet of the Apes*, looking into my cab window. He asked me what was it like to drive the taxi. I said it was very easy with such things as power steering and power brakes.

'It was a piece of cake,' I said, then asked him a question. 'What's it like driving a chariot being pulled by four enormous horses?' to which he replied, 'It was a piece of cake!' and we laughed. He told me he did not really drive the chariot, the stunt men did all the dangerous work and he did the slow bits. His long time wife was standing beside him and she laughed too. They were such a pleasant couple and asked what they should see in London. I said to see the best of London would require a lifetime. As they did not have a lot of time left in the capital, I recommended the Tate Britain. I would bet money that they really enjoyed that. Sadly, Charlton Heston died in 2008.

* * *

One day I dropped a passenger at Charing Cross Station. When the fare was paid I moved off slowly and immediately braked. They had left the door open. Normally there is an audible alarm but obviously it was not working that day. I had done a little damage to another car and quite a lot of damage to my cab door. The owner of the car told me not worry about it as her vehicle was just a pile of old junk. I was relieved to hear this. I did not want a big insurance claim against me.

This happened near the Queen Eleanor Memorial, which is just inside the station. There were twelve of these very ornate memorials erected by King Edward I in honour of his beloved wife. They started at the village of Harby in Nottinghamshire, and every day the funeral cortège rested, that spot was destined to have a memorial erected. The last one was at Charing Cross. Queen Eleanor was laid to rest in Westminster Abbey. Unfortunately, in 1671, Oliver Cromwell destroyed every one of these beautiful reminders of a King's lost love. The one at the station is an exact copy.

Charing Cross station was also the starting point for what became known as the Brighton Trunk Murders. In 1927, a corpse was found in a trunk at the left luggage department of Charing Cross station. Apparently the attendant noticed an extremely bad odour coming from a trunk and called the police. They opened it up and to their horror they discovered the torso of a woman. The legs and arms were cut from the body and separately wrapped in brown paper. These limbs were placed on top of the female torso in the trunk.

Seven years later, in 1934, the remains of a woman were found in a trunk at Brighton Station. The next day a case containing her legs was found at King's Cross Station. The police called in a man that I had mentioned earlier, the eminent police pathologist Sir Bernard Spillsbury, who had worked on the Dr Crippen case in 1910.

Eventually, the authorities traced the trunk to Brighton. When the police kicked down the door of 52 Kemp Street they found another trunk, which revealed another limbless female torso with all the outer extremities removed. The killer was one Tony Mancini, a heavy drinker, who was found not guilty of murder in 1934. In 1976, aged 68, he confessed to the *News of the World* but could not be tried again and so got away with his crime.

Chapter 28

There was a time when I was on a rank at the Conrad Hotel, near Chelsea Wharf. I was next in line when out came this guy of about twenty-five. A crowd of people ran towards him. He was quite good with these people and took the time to satisfy the fans with his autograph. He then came over to my cab and told me where he wanted to go. I said that I knew his face, but I could not put a name to it. He said, 'I am Nigel Mansell'. I apologised to him and said that I did not follow motor racing. I asked him if he would like to drive my cab but he declined my offer. Anyway it would have been illegal for him to drive a London cab, so it was an empty gesture.

Speaking of racing drivers, I used to see Stirling Moss quite regularly on a moped, riding up and down Park Lane. Every time I saw him he had a smile on his face. If he was in his racing car he would not have been moving very fast because of the traffic. What a difference between a speedy, souped-up car and a moped, but a moped is the best way to get around London, especially if you are in a hurry.

Chapter 29

As a television engineer in the seventies, I once went to Max Bygraves's flat in Victoria. He had had a very long run at the Victoria Palace Theatre and he strolled into our shop one morning and rented a very large colour television. I had to visit his flat quite few times, as these early sets were fairly unreliable. He would regularly ask his wife, Blossom, to make me a cup of tea while we were having a little chat. I would have preferred a couple of free tickets to his show, which was just around the corner, but the tickets never materialised. I thought that with a name like Bygraves he would have done well running a funeral parlour. (Just a joke.) Max was a very successful entertainer at that time and quite a jovial customer. I believe he emigrated to Australia, where his wife Blossom sadly died.

Bruce Forsyth was another television customer of ours. What a personality that guy had! He was with Anthea Redfern then, although I spoke with her for only a few minutes. What an attractive woman she was. She was on the Bruce Forsyth show and I do believe they got married in 1973. Bruce Forsyth starred in *Sunday Night at the London Palladium, The Generation Game* and since 2004, *Strictly Come Dancing*. What a career this guy has had, and he is still going strong. He was born in 1928, so that makes him 85.

* * *

Back on my cab crawl of memories round London, I remember driving into Liverpool Street Station where there was a big queue for taxis. When I picked up my passenger, he had a big cue in his hand. It was Terry Griffiths, the snooker player. Again I had to ask who he was. I admit, this sort of question can be a wee bit embarrassing. He had a nice but strong Welsh accent and was a great snooker player, but he took so long to take a shot. It was almost painful waiting, although when he eventually cued the ball it was usually pretty accurate.

* * *

Shirley Bassey was once one of our television customers. She was living in a house in Chester Square, possibly even the same house that Margaret Thatcher lives in at present. I remember the housekeeper let me in. As she walked me up a beautiful semi-circular white staircase I could see all of Shirley Bassey's number one gold hit awards. Each record was in the middle of its own frame with a small plaque just below the record that had all the relevant information. For every third step there was a gold disc award. It looked just like a Hollywood scene. The records included hits such as 'Goldfinger' and 'Big Spender'.

The second floor living room was palatial. There was a striking white grand piano in this Aladdin's cave, the lid lifted to show off its lines. Shirley Bassey was home but not seeing any one that day and I was a little upset about that.

Just as I was driving away from Chester Square I saw Tony Curtis standing on the corner of Eaton Square. One of his more famous movies was *Trapeze*. He was notable for his extremely black hair, which had gone completely grey. I would have preferred to see his gorgeous daughter, Jamie Lee Curtis. Belgravia is crawling with famous people.

* * *

At number 202 Bishopsgate, in the City of London, there is a public house called Dirty Dicks that dates back to 1875. Nearby there lived a certain Nathaniel Bentley. He was to be wed to the love of his life but sadly she died on the eve of their wedding. A broken-hearted Mr Bentley closed the wedding breakfast room, which was already prepared for the next day. He became a complete recluse until he died.

The empty house lay dormant for the next forty years. Eventually, the nearby pub purchased all of Bentley's effects, including the remains of a dried out old moggy, dusty, rusty old pots and pans complete with cobwebs, and put the lot on display. They then changed the name of the pub to Dirty Dicks. Soon it became a thriving, worldwide tourist attraction.

On one occasion my parents were visiting the pub to sample the ale and the atmosphere. My mother read the sign on the bar that said, 'Ask the barman to show you Dirty Dick's chamber'. She thought it meant his bed chamber and duly asked to see it.

Well! The barman slapped the biggest chamber pot that I have ever seen on the bar. My poor mum was a bit of a lady and she went completely red-faced, although she eventually joined in the laughter.

* * *

Speaking of dead cats, there is a dog cemetery in Hyde Park just to the right of the Victoria Gate lodge in Bayswater Road, which dates back to 1881. It is no longer in use. I found it sad to look through the railings and see these tiny gravestones scattered randomly about. They must have broken the hearts of their proud owners who have since joined them in heaven, or wherever we go when we leave this mortal coil.

It was never an official cemetery. A member of the gentry took along the remains of her dead dog, Cherry, a Maltese terrier, and the lodge keeper buried her in his garden. Soon word spread of a free canine cemetery. It closed in 1903, with a dog body count of about 300, with names like Chin Chin, Pupsey, Fairy, Bobbit and Scamp. The tiny cemetery gets overgrown every year and disappears under all the weeds. Luckily the Park's Commission give the place a good clean-up once a year. This gives the public a chance to view the tiny gravestones and feel the sadness that radiates from this tiny plot.

* * *

Back in my cab again and driving down Park Lane from Marble Arch, I spot a recently erected memorial wall to animals that were used in war. This monument is enormous. On either side of a concave wall there is a vast grass area where there are lifesize bronze statues of two pack horses, a dog and a mule. Many of the horses and mules sustained unreasonable treatment in times of war and I am sure they were all unwilling participants.

There are mentions of pigeons and canaries on the wall. These canaries were used to sniff out the deadly mustard gas in the 1914/18 War. If there was gas in the area, the poor old yellow bird keeled over, stone dead. It saved many lives, as it gave the soldiers time to don their gas masks. Canaries were widely used by coal miners in the mines to detect coal gas.

There is also a tribute to glow worms, believe it or not. A friend of mine known as Dublin Joe told me that a certain quantity were placed in a clean jam jar, the lid was screwed back on and the result is a kind of living torch that was used to light up maps, or newly arrived orders from the generals (who were at the rear of the battle). Incidentally, the glow worm is not a worm at all, it's the larvae of a beetle type bug.

I have repeatedly looked for the glow worms on the monument, but to no avail. Maybe they have gone to ground or the stone pigeons have scoffed the lot. The troops should have trained a nest of fireflies to hover over enemy positions in order to light them up, then the army gunners could see their target clearly. PS: I'm joking!

Chapter 30

Years ago, I remember a man coming to my cab window and asking me to take him to the Queen Elizabeth Hospital in Woolwich. I asked him was that anywhere near Ha-Ha Road.

Well, you should have seen his face. He thought that I was taking the mickey. So out comes my large print A to Z map and I show him a road running through Woolwich Common, quite near the hospital in question. He was a little bit apologetic, so I told him the story.

It all started at Kensington Palace when the head gardener wanted to keep out the public by separating Kensington Gardens from Hyde Park without spoiling the view by building a large wall. So he dug a deep ditch – in effect a sunken fence – and a very successful idea it was too. The public could not cross the deep ditch, and the Royals of Kensington Palace did not have their view spoilt. Every time the public saw this 'fence' they laughed, so the ditch became known as a ha-ha and the idea was copied all over the country.

The ha-ha at the Palace has long since gone but Ha-Ha Road, Woolwich really does exist and was built in 1774 to separate Woolwich Arsenal from the grazing fields on the common.

Chapter 31

In the eighties, I was called to a house in Eaton Place to repair a defective television. I saw a large blue plaque on the wall stating that Frederic Chopin, the Polish composer, lived here. (There is also a plaque to the composer Franz Liszt in London. I wonder if they ever went out together for groceries... Would they take a shopping list with them? A Chopin Liszt?)

Down the way we find Eaton Terrace, where Enoch Powell lived. He was born in the year that the *Titanic* was launched, 1912. He was the one that originally welcomed Caribbean immigrants to take the jobs that no one else wanted. Powell soon changed his mind and gave a very powerful speech about Rivers of Blood. I remember two Jamaican house painters from the building next door then sat down on Enoch Powell's front doorstep to eat their lunch every day for the next two weeks. They told me it was a silent protest. They were very nice guys and looked as if they had just stepped off the *Windrush*, the ship that carried the first wave of immigrants in 1948. Enoch never did ask the painters to move.

* * *

I once dropped off a beautiful, dark-skinned lady in Tavistock Square. She had a very strong Cockney accent that I fell in love with. She stood at the cab window waving a £20 note to pay the £5 fare and immediately I noticed it was a dud. I told her I would not accept this useless note and if she did not produce the correct cash I was going to stop a passing police car and they would cart her away. Like a magician, the correct fare was produced within seconds. She thanked me for not stopping the squad car and added that I could have passed the £20 onto my next fare. That would have been a criminal act that I would take no part in but as she walked away she gave me such a sexy smile that I instantly forgave her.

* * *

In my mind, as I drive away from Tavistock Square, I can see the memorial marking the spot where the terrible atrocity of 7/7 took place in 2005. The roof of a red double-decker bus was blown off and thirteen people were murdered. The perpetrator also took himself to heaven but I don't think they would let him in. There were other bombings on that fateful day and I remember it well. Just as the radio reported the atrocities, I was on my way to Heathrow with a fare, and no, he was not an escaping terrorist. I was glad to be getting out of London. On the evening news I saw a wrecked black cab right next to the blown-up bus. It could have been mine.

In the same square there is a blue plaque dedicated to Charles Dickens, who had yet another house here, before moving to Doughty Street to accommodate his growing family.

Beautiful, leafy Tavistock Square is also home to the British Medical Association, and there is a statue of Gandhi here holding a long staff and wearing a long white garment. Such a tiny, genteel man but he had a following of millions and changed the face of India.

* * *

A lady once left her handbag in my cab. Taxi drivers hate this as we have to go to a police station and spend a lot of earning time filling out unnecessary paper work. They count all the cash, lipsticks and all the stuff one would expect to find in a woman's handbag. They even counted the amount of Polo mints that were left in a half-used roll! This is, to my mind, just to annoy the cab driver.

One desk officer once asked me why I did not keep the property but that was a long time ago. It's all changed now. The Public

Carriage Office opened a dedicated Lost Property office at the upper end of Baker Street and a driver can now expect a ten per cent reward for the loss of his time due to the negligence of an absent-minded passenger.

* * *

A guy came out of the Cumberland Hotel and asked for the public house in Oxford Street. It's amazing that the world famous Oxford Street is one-and-three-quarter miles long, and has only one pub, The Tottenham, which has been there since 1790 (when it was known as The Flying Horse).

* * *

In my time as a cabbie I have made friends with my overseas passengers, especially from across the pond, and in particular one couple, a New York cop and his wife. His face was battered by violence and time, and he said he had been shot, stabbed, run over and even kidnapped during his twenty-nine year career in the NYPD (New York Police Department). Eventually he retired, studied law, and is now a top lawyer in Florida. They said that they would like to take me to dinner, so I recommended the Albert Pub in Victoria Street.

This ale house is a preserved building and cannot be pulled down or even altered. It is famous with foreign visitors. We were having a very tasty lunch when in comes a very large and intoxicated customer who started causing trouble. Immediately, up jumps our hero cop, gets him in an arm lock and bounces the thug straight out the door. He got a great clap from all the other customers. The landlord gave the three of us a free lunch plus complimentary drinks. The wife said that she had seen it all before. This ex-cop was seventy-two and looked like Ernest Borgnine. I would have loved to have gone out on patrol with this tough guy in his hey day, I bet it would have been better than the movies. But don't forget, one might have been shot dead, just for being there as an observer.

Chapter 32

Back on my cab tour, I remember being hailed by a punter in the City just outside what I thought was a bank counting house. We were joined by three other men who looked as if they were straight out of an *Indiana Jones* movie, all wearing trilby hats and trench coats. They loaded two large, trunk-type containers into my cab and directed me to a nearby City bank. When the containers were safely in the building, they asked me to take them back to the point of the original pick-up. I heard them whisper, 'Shall we tell him?' One of them said, 'Of course, why not?'

It turned out I had just delivered £4 million in £50 notes and cashable bonds. They said that we had been followed by a heavily-armed, unmarked police car. I really don't think they should have put me in such danger. After all, I was just a meagre cab driver, what if a robbery had been planned by thieves? I might have been an unwilling target. Even so, the tip was pretty good but the excitement of that day was priceless. I never found out why they used a London black cab but I got the distinct impression that the police had received a tip that there was going to be a hit on the regular security van.

Another time in the City I picked up a couple of hoodies – you know, the ones that wear their coat hoods up around their heads, even in the height of summer. They jumped into my cab at the traffic lights before I knew it, asking for a garage in Wandsworth. I knew this place and was friends with the owner, so I expected no trouble.

The big guys in the back were quite nice passengers. After they had paid me off from a bundle of £20 notes, they went on their way. It was then that I noticed a brown wallet lying on the floor of the cab. On examination, I saw it had a debit card and a City business card in a secret compartment. I assumed that the wallet had been pick-pocketed somewhere in the area where I had picked up my hoodies. It certainly had not been there when they boarded the taxi.

I phoned the number on the business card and the man on the other end had not even missed his wallet. He asked me to put the meter on and drive to his office. I do believe he suspected me at one stage but he must have asked himself why I would telephone him if I had stolen from him. He thanked me and gave me a nice shiny £20 note for my trouble but told me he had lost about £300 from the wallet – all in £20 notes...

* * *

A lovely Japanese couple once gave me a £50 note for a £5 fare. I ran after them. They were ever so grateful – so grateful, in fact, that they did not even give me a tip. Why am I so honest? It is probably down to my upbringing. Also, there could have been a candid camera hidden somewhere, you never know who is watching. It could have been a set-up, and if the cabbie succumbs to temptation, bang goes his cabbie licence.

Chapter 33

A long time ago, I was a heavy smoker who used to puff away at cigars, a pipe and at least thirty cigarettes per day. My twins said I smelled like a three-day-old, well-used ashtray. Anyway, about forty years ago I was called to do a television repair in the now closed Westminster Teaching Hospital on Horseferry Road. I was instantly brainwashed into giving up smoking. This is what happened.

I had successfully completed the repair of a colour television in the nurse's sitting room and as I was waiting for the imminent arrival of the lift I noticed a sign that had an arrow pointing the way to 'Morbid Surgery'. There were no people about because everybody had gone to lunch, and my curiosity pulled me in the direction of that arrow. I found myself in a room that frightened the living daylights out of me. There, on a special table, I could see a newly-removed set of human lungs. It was absolutely horrible. Nearby was a label that read 'These are the lungs of a fifty-five-year-old man who smoked most of his life'.

I could have picked up a piece of those black lungs and sprinkled it like pepper. The label went on to say, 'The damage was irreversible when he was alive. His death was totally brought about by a lifetime of non-stop smoking'. Next to those black lungs was a perfectly good set of lungs, put there as a comparison. The unfortunate person who owned the second set of lungs had died from some other terminal complaint.

That comparison must have thrown some sort of a switch deep in the back of my brain because I have not touched tobacco since, although I don't mind anyone smoking in my company. What a priceless and accidental cure.

There were also other exhibits on the table such as the shrivelled livers of some heavy drinkers. I admit that I enjoy a social drink or two and the shrivelled-up livers did not make me pack up drinking, but I am pretty careful these days about how much alcohol I consume.

For the next ten years I would stand in Horseferry Road, look up to the fourth floor window of that teaching hospital and see large preserving jars with human organs displayed in a solution of formaldehyde. The jars were in cabinets without backs and were framed in the windows, easily spotted from the road. They were not a pretty sight, and should not have been in the window for public viewing, even if they were on the fourth floor.

The hospital closed a few years later and was converted into prestigious flats, the jars now replaced by flowers and brightly coloured curtains. I don't think I would like to live in one of the fourth floor apartments. I might have nightmares of floating lungs and livers in the dead of night.

By the way, it's called Horseferry Road because it led to one of the few Thames ferry crossings for miles around. The first ferry was in 1513 and then Westminster Bridge was built in 1740, followed by an early version of Lambeth Bridge in 1862. This was the death knell for the ferrymen but the name of Horseferry Road has lived on, especially as the Horseferry Road Magistrates Court is well known to many convicted criminals.

A little bit further down the road toward the Houses of Parliament in Victoria Tower Gardens there is a reproduction of Auguste Rodin's statue, The Burghers of Calais, comprising five life-size bronze men in a semi circle, all in the dress of 1889. They seem to be whispering together. For all I know, they may even be whispering about my first book. I must say that for art lovers, this impressive gathering of bronze figures is worth a visit.

Their story is this: In the year 1347, King Edward III laid siege to the city of Calais. Starvation soon occurred within the city walls. Eventually, the King offered to spare everybody, provided that six city leaders emerged for execution. Eventually, six badly emaciated and hungry Burghers came out to be hanged, and in the nick of time, Queen Philippa of Hainault saved them by appealing to the king for clemency. Well known for her pity, this multiple statue was dedicated to Queen Philippa and her heart of gold.

* * *

William Huskisson was a Member of Parliament for Liverpool in the 1830s. He has the unusual reputation of being the first person to be killed on the railway. This unlucky man was opening a branch line out of Liverpool when he fell on to the tracks and was run over by none other than Stephenson's Rocket steam engine. There is a statue in Pimlico Gardens, Westminster, dedicated to this very unlucky man. God only knows why the statue shows him dressed in a Roman toga. More useless information, but it's fairly interesting, I must admit.

Chapter 34

As a television engineer, many strange things occur. I was doing a service call in a flat in Fitzrovia, a beautiful area full of continental restaurants quite near Tottenham Court Road tube station. I had been to this flat before and was fairly friendly with the tenants, a couple of lesbians whom I quite liked. One was fairly good looking but a little butch. The other was a very shapely blonde.

This particular day I was alone with the really attractive one in the flat. I was young then and fairly handsome, even though I say it myself, and also I was a bachelor. The tasty little piece was standing very close to me when suddenly she slapped a banger straight on my lips and it turned into a long, lingering kiss. Unfortunately it lingered a little too long. The door suddenly opened and in walked her large lover.

Well! This lady flew at me like a wild animal, grabbed me by my collar and shook me. This was a big girl and I was only ten-and-a-half stone. Suddenly she released my collar, and said, 'My friend has not fully made up her mind: is she, or isn't she?'

Then she added, 'Mind you, if I wasn't a lezzie I might also have given you a snog.' So I was let off the hook. Thank the Lord, I lived to snog another day.

These things happened quite often in the television service trade because one regularly met lonely housewives, widows and quite a lot of very flirty single females. I loved my work. It sounds as if I was a bit of a gigolo but I was never that, just a naive young man with little experience. Mind you, I was always willing to learn. I never went back to that flat but the memory of that kiss is still in my mind to this day. I wonder if the little blonde ever made up her mind as to whether she liked men or women? Mind you, she may have gone both ways.

* * *

Once I had a service call in a large house in Eaton Square. The lady of the house opened the door and I said I had come to repair her television set. This very elegant lady said the tradesmen's entrance was round the back in the mews. I enquired as to where the telly was and she pointed to the front room, which was only a couple of yards away. I would have had to drive around three streets to get to the mews in question and then walk through the kitchen and various corridors to get back to where I was standing at the front door. So I dove straight back to our service department and told them the story. Two days later the posh lady rang the firm and asked, 'Where is the engineer, I have not been able to watch television for two days.'

This lady was told that she had not let the repairman in and we could not send another man for at least another couple of days. Actually, we were not very busy at that time but the firm backed me one hundred per cent. The day of the tradesman's entrance had died out after World War II.

Chapter 35

On my mythical cab journey, I have been talking a lot about Belgravia, Westminster and Knightsbridge. The Duke of Westminster owned most of these areas until fairly recently, when a law was passed that forced him to sell some of his property. The family date back quite a few hundred years. I had a tour of Cheshire once – his family home, Eaton Hall, is in this county. As the coach passed through a through a small village, the driver told us that it was owned by the Duke of Westminster. He went on to say that sometime during the seventeenth century (although it could have been later), the Duke was riding his horse through this village and the men who were drinking outside the pub did not lift their caps to show respect. In anger, the Duke had the pub closed down and to this day there is still no public house in this village. This was how the gentry behaved in those days. Today they are a finer breed of men and women, and they respect us peasants now. I think.

On this tour, we visited a church near the village, which was probably also owned by the Duke, and were shown some gravestones. The headstones all said that the interned corpses had been buried in linen. Apparently, at some stage the linen cloth trade had started to flounder, the mills were failing and a new law was created, stating that at all funerals the undertaker must arrange for the deceased to be wrapped in linen. What a way to save a trade from going bust! We should pass a new law today stating that all corpses be dressed in newly-bought clothes in order to meet their Maker. This would help some of the struggling tailors, cobblers and milliners clamber out of the recession. The tradespeople could even advertise on the side of the coffin. Is that enterprising or what?

* * *

In an earlier chapter I wrote about Sweeney Todd, the demon barber of Fleet Street, who had an evil trapdoor under his barber's chair. Oddly enough there was a similar episode of customer murder in the Ostrich Inn in Colnbrook, near Heathrow. This inn is the third oldest public house in the land. It is supposed to be haunted because in the seventeenth century, some sixty travelling guests were murdered in one particular bedroom over a period of time. A device had been attached to the bed and a trap door was opened, tipping the poor old sleeping guest down into the kitchen and into an extremely large vat of boiling water. The victim was dead instantly – just like the killing of a lobster – and the unfortunate traveller's belongings were then pilfered. The landlord, one John Jarman, and his evil wife, were hanged for these heinous deeds.

Interestingly, I do not expect the builders knew what an ostrich was when the pub was originally erected in the twelfth century. Some say it was probably a distortion of the words 'oyster bridge'.

Chapter 36

In the early seventies, the television firm that I worked for developed a mobile workshop that would promote the television rental business's quick service and all that went with it. The vehicle had its own generator so that television sets could be repaired on board the vehicle. It looked like a red ice-cream van and had a drop flap at the side, just like Mister Softee's triple cone van. One day, a kid actually came to the van and asked for an ice cream. The lad was so disappointed when I said, 'We have no ice cream'. The boy's mother was not very happy either.

Anyway, my driver and I were sent to a Luton fair to show off the new service van and Harry H Corbett and Wilfred Bramble were there to promote their show, *Steptoe and Son*. They actually came into our service van and we had such a great laugh. They are both dead now but I was so proud to meet these two hilarious actors.

As we were in Luton for the weekend my colleague and I had to book into a hotel for the night. We were given an expense account, so we both went to the local hop, where I met a girl that worked for the Luton Hoo country estate. We had a few dances and a few drinks together and we got on pretty well. Then she said she had a moped parked outside and I replied, foolishly, that I could drive the bike with her on the back.

What I did not realise was that the bike was an automatic, and when I kick started the machine, off it went on its own. I had to run with it, holding tight on to the handlebars in sheer panic. The girl started running on the other side of the bike. She was screaming, and shouting, 'Mind my bike, mind my bike. It's not paid for yet'. I didn't know how to stop the thing, it was like a scene from a *Carry On* movie. Eventually, we got the machine under control and she jumped onto the bike, looked me straight in the eyes and said rather aggressively 'Goodbye', before riding off, leaving me there all alone. It was all very embarrassing. I had just been dumped by a raging girl on a moped and I did not even know where my hotel was.

* * *

On Chelsea Embankment one day in 1985, I was hailed by a colourful American Red Indian chief. I was just about to say 'How' (as in the Red Indian greeting) but stopped myself in time – he may have thought I was being rude. Anyway, he pointed across the Thames to the Peace Pagoda in Battersea Park, and said, 'I go there'. It was a command from a real Indian warrior.

During the journey he said he was a fund-raiser for these worldwide monuments. The Peace Pagoda houses an enormous gold Buddha in the classic cross-legged sitting position. The Buddha is Japanese although I was told those who built it in 1985 were Tibetan and actually lived in the park in makeshift tents. These unpaid builders were men of religion who lived on their wits plus handouts from the public, because as sincere vegetarian Buddhists they had absolutely no money. In those days you could always find them at the Covent Garden fruit and vegetable market in Nine Elms, where they foraged for thrown-away food at the close of market trading. Even to the present day you can always find a monk in attendance at the Peace Pagoda – I suppose he is some sort of unpaid permanent caretaker. The Japanese – and the Tibetans – are such well-cultured people.

When the taxi fare was paid, I got out of the cab to have a stretch. This is a very serene and mentally rewarding place and I recommend a trip to this holy shrine if you ever want total peace of mind. It's a good thing that I hung around. My fare only asked me to take him to Heathrow afterwards – a fare of £18, which was a lot of money in those days. What a result.

Battersea Park was not always there. It was opened in 1858 and before that it had been fertile marshland where they grew lavender for the perfume industry. These marshy fields ran all the way up to what is now called Lavender Hill, in Clapham. At the time they were clearing the Battersea marshlands they were also constructing the docks in East London, so they used barges to move all the excavated clay from the docks to Battersea Park. One could say Battersea Park was imported from East London.

In 1951, Battersea Park opened the Festival of Britain, held to boost the low morale of the people who had been through two devastating world wars. The Festival was extremely successful and attracted hordes of people from all over the world. The Pleasure Gardens in the northern part of the park included a great funfair with a big rollercoaster, a tree walk, a water chute and lots of great stuff to amuse the excited punters. In 1972, one of the rollercoaster cars lost its grip on the holding rail at the very top of the ride and started to roll backwards, with devastating consequences. Five children were killed and 13 seriously injured. The amusements declined in popularity after this and the funfair was closed in 1974.

Today Battersea Park is really worth a visit. Take the kids. There is a lovely zoo for children with all sorts of beasties. There is a pump house that has lots of art displays, where they perform marriage ceremonies 'by arrangement only'. And don't forget to have a look at the famous Guinness Clock. Battersea Park is a hidden gem waiting to be discovered. I have even seen the Henry Moore statues, Three Standing Figures, here.

Moore made his name by casting huge, distorted figures of animals and human beings in bronze, which are mostly on loan to various parks. I remember I was driving through Hyde Park on the day that he died in 1986. I saw all the Moore exhibits being taken away on low loaders, probably on the orders of the executors of his will. These abstract sculptures were, and still are, priceless.

Chapter 37

Over the years, I have taken quite a lot of long weekend breaks by coach, mostly to Eastbourne, Brighton and other coastal resorts. One of my very best trips was to a sixties and seventies party weekend. They can be fantastic but this depends on how lively the other guests are. I was lucky on one such trip in 2007 as I was the only male on the coach alongside forty-two females, and I must say they were the most wonderful crowd of partygoers I have ever met. I had the time of my life on that particular weekend.

Usually the coach parties come from all over the United Kingdom. I have found that people from the North are always full of beans. As the coach picks up its passengers they are mostly strangers but by the time they arrive at the hotel, everybody knows who's who. It's lovely to meet such people. All they want is a good time.

During one of these trips to Eastbourne I took the Saturday bus to Brighton for the day. I adore this lively city, it seems to radiate the good life after a couple of pints of Old Wallop on the shoreline board walk, a great meal and a good earful of busking near the pier. (And don't forget the hordes of beautiful ladies, most of them three sheets to the wind, down for weekend hen parties.)

When it was time for me to get my bus back to Eastbourne I headed in the direction of the bus stop, passing the side of the Royal Pavilion. It was then that I heard the singing of angels coming from a small concert room at the side of this extremely ornate building. A sign read, 'Free Choral Concert today'.

I was pulled into the auditorium like a pin to a magnet by the angelic vocals of a choir of beautiful women, The Shoreham Singers, all wearing long black flowing dresses. At the time I was mourning the loss of my wife in 2008 and was extremely emotional. The song they were singing was called 'The Emptiness Still Bears the Traces of You'. Well! Do try reading those words again and try to understand their full meaning. Even now I feel sad again as I write this.

As I stood quite near to this heavenly choir, a few tears crept into my eyes. A grey-haired man with a kind face came over and said, 'Are you OK, mate?' I told him the song reminded me of my wife. This man, who was about seventy or eighty, introduced me to the composer of the song. The kind man's name was Herbie Flowers and he had written the song 'Grandad' for Clive Dunn.

Herbie also co-founded the groups Blue Mink and Sky. He played some of the music for the film *The War of the Worlds* and he has appeared alongside many well-known musicians such as Tom Jones, Frank Sinatra, George Harrison, T. Rex, Elton John, Led Zeppelin and David Bowie. I was so lucky to meet such a polite and talented character that day. Herbie Flowers plays the bass guitar, the piano and the tuba and was even kind enough to e-mail me the beautiful song that had brought tears to my eyes. I could keep writing about this accomplished musician forever, but I must move on.

Chapter 38

Now we go back to London. There is a famous hat shop in St James's Street called Lock & Co, which has been there since 1676. The present shop window probably dates back to the 1800s and I am sure the interior decor has not changed either. The shop once received a postcard from abroad and the only words on the envelope were: 'The best hatters in the world, London.' The letter was promptly delivered to number six St James's Street. Admiral Lord Nelson, Sir Winston Churchill, Charlie Chaplin and various kings, dukes, and princes all had their hats made to measure in this shop. I bet they still have some of the original head measurements of these famous people.

A story in circulation is that Lewis Carroll, the writer of *Alice in Wonderland*, got his mad hatter story from this shop. Apparently the hatmakers went a bit loony from inhaling the fumes of the chemicals used in the production of these expensive hats. Also, the internal metal rim transferred dangerous particles of lead into the brain of the wearer and over the years it caused a bit of mental disorder. So you had mad hat makers *and* mad hat wearers. Lead is known to be extremely dangerous to the human body but these days, safety standards are much higher.

A few doors down from number six we come to Berry Bros wine house. Above this shop existed the Texas Embassy to the Court of St James in 1836. Then there were a few battles between Mexico and the United States, the US won and the Texas embassy ceased to exist. The rooms are still there and so is the original flagpole. My American passengers loved this very obscure but true story. Out came the cameras as usual and up went the tip.

If you walk down Pall Mall you will arrive at Cockspur Street where there is a large restaurant called the Texas Embassy Cantina. This building was once owned by the White Star Line, a major shipping company that owned the famous Titanic. It was on these premises that they sold the first, and of course, the last tickets for the maiden voyage of that doomed liner. I mentioned this ship in an earlier chapter – it was a 'one liner' for George Best. There is a hidden joke in there somewhere.

Down the side of Berry Bros is a very narrow passageway leading to Pickering Place and a sign on the side that tells its story. This is the smallest square in Great Britain and dates back to 1531, during the reign of King Henry VIII. Just before they built the square there was a nuns' leper colony on the site. It seems there was quite a lot of leprosy in medieval days. The very last duel with swords was fought to the death in this square. Soon after, duelling was outlawed. Gambling dens, bear baiting, dog fighting and bare knuckle fighting could also be found in this low-life square but today the place is extremely upmarket and tranquil. The original Georgian houses are still there and are hugely expensive.

At the bottom of St James's Street is St James's Palace, where King Charles I walked to his execution. As it was a cold day, the king asked for extra clothing to stop him shivering, worried that the onlookers might think he was shaking with fear. He was a man with great courage and dignity.

Driving to the top of St James's Street, we cross over Piccadilly into Albemarle Street where we find Browns Hotel. This is where Alexander Graham Bell demonstrated his new invention, the telephone. Apparently he rang Buckingham Palace where a telephone had been installed and spoke to Queen Victoria. It is written that she said to Bell, 'We are not amused'.

* * *

I was on the Hilton Hotel rank in Park Lane when two American media men came out and asked to be taken to Doris Stokes.

This lady was a fairly famous medium on the telly many years ago. She claimed to be able to talk to the dead and read people's minds from a distance. 'OK,' I said, 'Can I have the address?' She lived somewhere out in the sticks. The Yanks said they had heard that all London cab drivers knew everything. I was lost for words. 'Can you not contact her mentally, or better still, give her a ring?' I asked them. So they rang this lady and she lived thirty miles out of town, and off we went.

* * *

You never know who is going to emerge from these top hotels. I picked up Buzz Aldrin's wife once who chatted to me about her famous spaceman husband. They were the astronauts on Apollo 11 – Aldrin was the second man to step on the lunar surface, Neil Armstrong being the first. Is it not uncanny that the mother of the second man to walk on the moon had the maiden name of Marion Moon? Sadly, Aldrin was not in London at the time. I would have loved to have met him, he might have brought me back a cheese sandwich from the lunar surface!

Another time, probably in the late eighties, I spoke to Tom Jones. He was not as tall as I expected. Mr Jones was dressed in running gear, heading for the 'green, green grass' of Hyde Park for a jog. This amazing Welsh singer has given pleasure to millions of lovers on the dance floors all over the world and he radiated one of the strongest personalities I have ever experienced. Well, most Welsh people do, don't they? Mr Jones could have been an opera singer, he certainly had the voice, and he also had the courtesy to speak to anybody that wanted to have a little chat. That is a rare quality, is it not?

On another occasion, I was on the rank outside the Inn on the Park in Park Lane when Amir Khan the boxer came out to show off his newly won champions belt. It was a world title belt and the trophy was nearly as big as Khan was. Again, another pleasant kind of a guy.

Chapter 39

About twenty years ago, I was on my way to Mitre Square in the City with a teenage female passenger. When we arrived at our destination I wanted to tell this young girl what had happened in this square but it was dark and I did not want to frighten her. However, this was one of the murder sites of Jack the Ripper. In 1888, the mutilated body of Catherine Eddows was discovered in this square. Her reproductive organs and other vital bits had been removed.

Not far away is the Ten Bells public house. It was in this pub that Annie Chapman had her last drink. Apparently she left the pub and turned right into Hanbury Street, only to be butchered by an unknown assailant. Jack was the only suspect.

Jack the Ripper's last victim was Mary Kelly from Limerick, and she was the most mutilated of all his victims. She was found in her bed, the main part of her stomach and reproductive system removed and other organs strewn all over the room. Both her breasts had been sliced off and placed on the mantelpiece. There is very little evidence that Mary was a prostitute and her grave can be seen in St Patrick's Roman Catholic graveyard in Leytonstone, East London. Flowers appear on her grave every year. Who is that person who leaves flowers to someone who died over 120 years ago, I wonder? Weird, is it not.

I met some Americans who were keen on the gruesome activities of Jack, so I took them to the Ten Bells public house. It was closed at the time but the landlord saw my cab and let us in for a private view. It was like walking into the past, you could feel the atmosphere of more than one hundred years ago. This is where some of Jack's victims supped their ale and gin. All of my passengers were in awe, they had never seen a place like it. This pub was used in two films about Jack the Ripper, one with Johnny Depp and the other for television with Michael Caine, both playing police inspector Frederick Abberline. The film people did not have to change much of the pub decor for the films because it looks exactly the same as it did 120 years ago.

The stories about a letter written in blood and the kidney sent through the post to the police were all hype. These stories were written by the editors of their own newspapers to boost the circulation. Many theories exist as to who the killer was but no one knows the answer and I think no one ever will, unless someone invents a time machine.

* * *

In 1888, London was the largest city in the world. It is written that there were well over 1,000 known prostitutes in the Whitechapel slum area at that time. People were so poor they had nowhere to sleep. A double bed in a lodging house cost three pennies, a single bed cost tuppence, and the worst off paid a penny to hang on a rope. A number of ropes were strung from one wall to the opposite side of a room and people would fall asleep with both arms slung over the rope and their feet on the ground. If you were tired you would sleep anywhere. It must have been some sight to see all those human beings hanging on a rope fast asleep. It reminds me of a washing line for tired people, or puppets on a string.

* * *

I remember the time a lady came to my cab window and said to me 'lonesome?' I shook my head and said, 'Well, maybe a little bit'. She then said, 'No, I want the place called Lonesome, near Streatham'. Well, after all my years driving a cab I had never heard of this place, so out comes my A to Z and there it was, just as she said. What a weird name for a place. I have since been asked for Snodland in Kent, and a place well out of town called Ugley, in Essex. Talking of weird names, there are two more I must mention: Upper Dicker and Lower Dicker, in East Sussex. What sort of a person named these twin villages? I have just heard that the UK town called 'Dull' has been unofficially twinned with a town in America called 'Boring'. How about that!

* * *

The Irish Embassy is at Seventeen Grosvenor Place. This building was a gift from the Guinness Family to the Irish Government. The number seventeen is very appropriate, as St Patrick's Day falls on 17th March.

Just across the road is the rear wall of Buckingham Palace. In 1982, a man called Michael Fagan infiltrated the grounds, climbed up a drainpipe and entered the royal residence. He parked himself on the Queen's throne, drank her wine and then sat on the side of the monarch's bed and chatted with her for nearly an hour before the police arrived. What a blunder for the royal bodyguard. Mr Fagan had no intention of harming the Queen, in fact he adored Her Majesty.

Since then, the Queen's protection has been well and truly beefed up but a few years later I saw a group of women activists place a ladder on the same wall, climb it and drag another ladder up to the top of the newly-laid barbed wire. They were in the grounds before the police arrived but they were all arrested pretty quickly.

* * *

I have been speaking quite a lot about the stars and other heavenly bodies that I have met. Look to the sky at night. This is what Patrick Moore did, and made a great living out of it. In 1957, Moore started presenting *The Sky at Night*, a monthly programme on astronomy. I believe the programme is still going, making it the world's longest running television series with the same presenter. He is now eighty-nine.

I picked Mr Moore up once and took him to a London University where he was going to give a lecture on astronomy. Patrick Moore told me he was a PT instructor in the RAF. He told me about the time he was a young man and two six-foot thieves set out to rob him. It was such a mistake for them. He walked away leaving the two would-be robbers lying unconscious on the pavement. They had picked on the wrong man. Sir Patrick Alfred Caldwell-Moore, to give him his full name, looked like an unmade bed on the passenger seat of my cab. He was wearing the most ill-fitting blue suit that I have ever seen. He was chairman of the now disbanded anti-immigration United Country party.

* * *

I remember I had just completed a repair on a television set in Bickenhall Mansions off Baker Street and was in the lift with a ten-year-old girl on the way to the ground floor. Suddenly the lift stopped and all the lights went out. It was total darkness. I was feeling a little uneasy when out of the dark silence came a calm little voice saying, 'Don't worry, the power will come back on for thirty seconds, it will be long enough for the lift to get us to the ground. It has happened before. Do trust me.' It was like my guardian angel had appeared in the darkness of the lift. Even though I could not see the little girl I felt reassured, and sure enough, on came the lights and the lift moved to the ground floor. The doors opened and the girl walked out of the lift and said, 'Told you so'. She then disappeared, not knowing the mental relaxation that she had given to me.

Margaret Thatcher was Prime Minister at that time and Arthur Scargill was the main union leader and they literally agreed on nothing. Thatcher's famous statement to Scargill was 'There will be no beer and sandwiches at Downing Street'. I thought it was a bit disrespectful.

There was lots of unrest. The miners were on strike in 1984–5, causing severe power cuts almost every day, hence the lift incident. The mounted police were a little heavy handed on the picket lines and there were lots of pictures of bloodied miners being shown on the television. Some mining villages became ghost towns and families had to move to other towns. But it's all history now.

Chapter 40

In 1935, the previous German embassy stood at Nine Carlton House Terrace, just off Pall Mall. This was when the Nazi Party was in full swing in Germany. Dr Leopold von Hoesch was the ambassador to Britain. When his German Shepherd dog Giro died, Hoesch had him buried under a tree just outside number nine. After World War I, the Americans and the British refused to call the breed a German Shepherd, so the authorities reverted back to the place from where the animal originated, namely Alsace. Hence, the German Shepherd was renamed the Alsatian. As for Dr von Hoesch, he was never a Nazi sympathiser. The dog's tomb stone reads, 'Giro, Ein Treuer Begleiter.' Translated it reads, 'Giro, A true companion.'

People still call his pet 'the Nazi dog' and even now there are remnants of the Nazis in this old embassy. Top Nazi architect Albert Speer redesigned some of the interior and a marble staircase was said to have been donated by the evil fascist Mussolini. Apparently there is a mosaic of swastikas on the floor of one of the public rooms. However, Hoesch was so well respected in London that in 1936 they gave him a full state funeral with a nineteen-gun salute.

* * *

I have just returned from a weekend in Folkestone, where I met a man from Redcar who said he lived in a council house opposite Sir Stanley Matthews (1915–2000). He told me that when Mr Matthews got his invitation to Buckingham Palace to collect the gong that would make him a Sir, the locals had to have a whip round to buy him a new suit for the occasion.

I find it extremely difficult to believe this story, especially when Sir Stanley had played football all over the world. He was one of England's greatest players and was known as the 'wizard of the dribble.' I know that footballers' wages then were only a tiny fraction of today's earnings but if he was living in a council house I am sure that Stoke City or Blackpool would surely have looked after him. I wish I knew the true story.

That weekend at Folkestone included a coach tour. We were passing Beachy Head in East Sussex when the driver told us this was one of the United Kingdom's favourite suicide hotspots. He went on to say that up until about two years ago, the suicide rate was about sixty sad people every year but because of the recession the numbers had risen to 160 jumpers per annum, although I can't confirm this. Beachy Head is rated number two in the world's suicide count. The world's number one is the Golden Gate Bridge in California.

The coach driver took us to a tiny old church in Winchelsea called St Thomas the Martyr, where he pointed out the grave of Spike Milligan, who started the Goons with Peter Sellers, Harry Secombe and Michael Bentine. These words are written on his tombstone in Gaelic, 'Duirt me leat go raibh me breoite'. It translates in English to, 'I told you I was ill'. The Diocese of Chichester insisted that the inscription should be written in the Irish language. I think they did it so that visitors to the graveyard would not be able to understand the words on Spike's gravestone and therefore would not laugh in this solemn place. Milligan sure had a great sense of humour. There is a blue plaque to him in a street just off the Bayswater Road.

Our tour coach then went to the ancient village of Ditchling, home to Dame Vera Lynn, the Forces' sweetheart in World War II. Dame Vera is now ninety-five and still going strong. Ditchling dates back to the year 765 AD and is only nine miles from Brighton. They have a wonderful male and female choir called the 'Ditchling Singers', formed by the brilliant Herbie Flowers who I mentioned earlier and who also lives in the village.

We also took a trip to the East Sussex village of Peasmarsh. It suffered from the bubonic plague in the fourteenth century. In the eighteenth century there lived a vicar in this village who had a son called Charles Dodgson, better known as the author with the pen name of Lewis Carroll, who wrote *Alice in Wonderland*. Apparently the Alice of the title was a local lass. Sir Paul McCartney owns a large estate nearby.

Chapter 41

When I first came to London from Ireland as a qualified radio and television engineer in the late fifties, I was offered a job with a hearing aid firm in Acton. I actually repaired the hearing aid that belonged to the fifties singer Johnnie Ray, who became almost completely deaf after surgery in 1958. He could have fixed the hearing aid himself as all that was wrong with it was wax blocking the tube that enters the ear hole. It was a horrible job, as human wax smells. Ray had hits in America with 'Just Walkin' in the Rain', 'The Little White Cloud That Cried', 'Such a Night' and lots of rock 'n' roll music in the fifties and sixties. I never met Johnnie Ray as I left the firm the day before he came to collect his deaf aid. To this day I still love his music.

There was an experimental factory next door and I was invited in to see their brand new invention, a computer. They took me into a room that housed the device, which took up every available space in the room. There were banks of small glass valve-operated equipment everywhere and the heat was unbearable. This was one of the forerunners of the modern day computer.

Eventually the transistor was invented, and I even remember the number on that small device, the 'OC7O'. It was used mainly in the new portable receivers called the transistor radio, affectionately known as the tranny. A changing breed of kids emerged during that era. They found a new freedom, and took these small portable radios with them everywhere they went, mostly tuned into Radio Luxemburg. All the teenagers adored this new listening apparatus. It's strange to be able to remember the number of that first transistor device, especially now that fifty-five years have elapsed.

The old fashioned thermionic valve radios and televisions had had their day, they went to museums and were put on display so that future generations could stare and say, 'Look at the size of those tellys and radios'.

After the transistor came the solid state silicon chip. Today's computers can be put into a pocket and you can hang fifty-inch television sets on the wall that are just two inches thick. Years ago you would have to go into a phone box to make a call, nowadays the phone 'box' fits in a handbag. That's what you call progress. There is no limit to man's creativity. I suppose the term, 'Beam me up, Scotty,' is not as daft as it sounds and one day it may become a reality. I was born fifty years too soon.

All those years ago, I remember converting a hearing aid into a small transistor radio that fitted into a fairly small soap box and worked with a tiny ear piece. I lent the device to an employee in the factory. He never gave the radio back but a month later I saw a very similar radio in a gadget shop window in Tottenham Court Road. It was a copy of my radio. I am convinced my idea was stolen, and there was nothing I could do about it.

I also recall the time I was approached by one of the union leaders at the factory to bug the manager's office. I was reluctant to do this but I did show him how to do the bugging. For some reason or other the guy was sacked a week later, which I was quite pleased about. Apparently the union chap never got around to fitting the bug in the manager's office. It would not have worked anyway as I did not tell him the proper way to install it, deliberately leaving out a few details. This was to protect myself from an expensive prosecution should I have been found out.

As I got older, everything started changing at an unbelievable rate and I lost the will to keep up with the new technology. It was obvious I did not have enough brain capacity to keep pace with all the new equipment that was appearing on the horizon and that's when I decided to become a black cab driver. I soon found

out that I would need twice the brain capacity to complete The
Knowledge of London. I have written about that episode in
previous pages.

Chapter 42

Now I must take a quick mental trip across the Irish Sea. For some unknown reason my parents decided to set up home in Belfast. I still had a few years to go to become a teenager. Northern Ireland was not a good place to be at that particular time. World War Two was close to its final conclusion. Victory was imminent, but at a great sacrifice. I remember the extremely large barrage balloons in the sky, and the batteries of very noisy ACAC guns that were trying to shoot the last remnants of the German Luftwaffe out of the sky. I have a vivid recollection of the gigantic search lights illuminating these remaining bombers. I have actually seen a rare flying boat land in what I think was Belfast Loch. What a sight to behold.

And then the war was suddenly over. Hitler was dead. Suicide it was called, and well overdue if I may say so. I remember the street parties, we were actually given real food. I still cannot forget the flavours of all that meat, ice cream, plus the odd banana or orange – remember, we had very little to to eat then.

The streets of Belfast were packed with well heeled, and well polished American soldiers, there were air men and navy men, mostly in civilian clothes, looking like film stars. They were all up for a good time. The streets of Belfast looked just like a 1940s film set, but these were no actors, this was the real thing. They had the cash, the nylons, the chocolate, the chewing gum, and the overwhelming desire to mingle with the local women. This caused a little friction with the returning British servicemen. The Yanks had all the glitter, and the locals did not have the flashy uniforms or the sheer nylons to charm the starry-eyed ladies. I, as a young lad, felt sincerely sorry for the British Tommy, who could not compete with all this overwhelming Yankee glamour.

* * *

Eventually my parents made the decision to return to the Republic of Ireland. We settled in one of the most beautiful towns that I have ever lived in. It was a place called Malahide, just nine miles from Dublin. It had its own castle, its own beach, and three pubs. I spent my time swimming every day, climbing trees and fishing. We had real summers then that lasted from April through to September.

One day a dead body was washed into the bay. He was naked, but my great pal and I noticed he had a gold ring on his finger. We were determined to steal that beautiful piece of digit adornment. Apparently, the poor old deceased guy had been to the Baldoyle races, and had lost all his wages on the gee-gees. So, with the usual help of alcohol and depression, the fellow jumped into the sea to end it all. The undercurrents of the sea were deadly around that turbulent coast. This poor man would not have lasted very long in those churning waters. And so he ended up being washed ashore on the Malahide coast.

In those days there were no such things as mortuaries in Malahide. So the cadaver was laid out on an old wooden table in a disused garage behind the police station. This was called temporary storage. My friend and I were present at the overnight interment. The two Garda Siochana (Police) did not even tell us to get lost.

In the dead of night, my pal and I crept towards the makeshift mortuary. The scene was extremely eerie. Slowly we opened the door. It was then that the full moonlight shone directly on to the pure white face of the deceased. Well, what was left of one eye was hanging from its socket and down the side of the poor fellow's face. I do believe it was the crabs that had eaten most of it. The other eye was wide open, and staring directly at me and my friend. It was the horrible stare of death.

105

We were frozen stiff with fear. It was just like a scene from one of the Hammer House of Horror movies. Eventually, when we were able to get our legs to move, we ran like swiftest deer in peril, just to get away. You know, I can still see that poor man's face to this present day, but that awful image no longer bothers me. How stupid we were then.

There was another time when my pals and I foolishly decided to remove the flag from the battlements of the ever so beautiful Malahide castle. We all met after dark and trekked through the woods to the castle. Luckily there was scaffolding going up the side to the flat roof. So up we went. At the top we made our way towards the flag pole. It was then that a door opened, and a very threatening voice shouted 'Who's there?' The man then let off two barrels of a shot gun into the air. It was very dark but we all made it in quick time back to the scaffolding, shinnied down the poles, and disappeared into the woods. The next day we were called to the police station to receive a good telling off. I believe that one of our gang was recognised, and must have divulged all of our names to the police.

My mother or father had never physically punished me up until then. A very strong glare was enough to put me back in my place. But that was the day they gave me a good hiding to remember. It was then that I grew up mentally. The worst thing was that my mother was a regular chatter to Lady Talbot, the lady of the castle. This genteel woman always took her daily walk past our house, and always passed the time of day with my mother. My mum was very embarrassed by my crazy actions on the castle roof. But that's all part of growing up. It's strange to think that one of my Christian names is 'Talbot' but I'm definitely not related to the Talbots of the castle.

* * *

My parents are buried in the local graveyard. Just a few graves along lie the victims of a terrible mass murderer. Six in all were brutally attacked and slain in what was known as the La Mancha murders. Two brothers, two sisters, and two workers in this large mansion house were all beaten to death. The jury found a man called Henry McCabe guilty of this evil crime. He was eventually hanged at Mountjoy jail. It's sad that whenever I visit my parents' grave I always have a walk along to the La Mancha mass grave, and give a little thought to those poor souls who violently lost their lives way back in 1926.

We used to drink in a country pub in Kildare which had a very long glass display case that contained a gruesome severed human arm. It was black from age, and belonged to a seventeenth century pugilist. He had the longest arms in the history of boxing. This man could tie the laces of his breeches without even bending. Laces in those old type breeches were always below the knees. His name was Dan Donnelly, he was never defeated in any of his heavyweight fights. It appears that this was due to the unusual length of his arms, because no one could get anywhere near him in order to smack his jaw. After his death, one of this man's arms was removed by a surgeon, pickled in alcohol, then varnished and put on display. 'What a finish the arm had' (in more ways than one). The local constabulary were not very pleased. All fights were bare knuckle then. Soon, John Douglass, the then Marquess of Queensberry, endorsed the new rules of boxing. This meant that from then on boxers had to wear gloves, thus reducing the possibility of brain damage. To this day the Marquess of Queensberry Rules still apply to all boxing. Dan Donnelly's time was 1788 to 1820.

I hated going to church on Sundays. It was the odour of unwashed parishioners at the time. Few people had baths, although we did have a bathroom. It was that time when things were beginning to get better for everyone. I remember the priests used to preach 'Hell and Damnation' in the pulpit, and later they could be found in the Grand Hotel downing double whiskies and eyeing up the women guests, whilst the men of the parish would mostly head to one of the three local pubs, and by the time they went home for their Sunday dinner they were mostly three sheets to the wind. They just fell asleep. Those days are gone now, and men are more respectful to their spouses. I do believe there is more harmony in the home. I do hope that I am correct on this fragile marital subject, after all, 'I was married twice'.

* * *

I suppose I am lucky to be alive after I relate the next incident that happened in my past. I was always a bit of a beachcomber in my youth. The best time to walk and comb the beach was just after a great storm, as this was usually followed by a very high tide that washed all sorts of flotsam and jetsam on to the sandy beach.

After one particular stormy evening I headed for the shore line and started my search for whatever the waters had thrown up, and there it was, just lying there. It was a World War Two German incendiary bomb. I did not know what I had found at the time, so I picked up the device and took it straight to the police station. I walked in to the cop shop, and put the bomb down on the desk. Well, I have never seen policemen move so fast, they even dragged me into the street with them. Apparently the bomb was live, and had to be disarmed by the bomb squad. They told me how lucky I had been that day. I could have been instantly roasted like an ox.

I am now nearly finished my Irish contribution to this book, so just a few more words and then I'm off back to the place that I love best, London.

I really remember Dublin in the rare old times. Nelson's Pillar was a great meeting place for all Dubs. It stood like a giant obelisk in the centre of O'Connell Street, which is one of the widest city streets in Europe. Incidentally, the longest street in Europe is in Muldova near Romania. 'What a piece of useless information,' ah, but not on a quiz night. The Pillar was a great place to be, it was the national landmark. When the IRA blew it up, it fell straight down the middle of O'Connell Street with very little damage. A stump was left, so the Army blew that up, apparently causing a lot of collateral damage to the surrounding area. The council installed a beautiful bronze statue of Queen Maeve, a legendary Iron Age warrior queen, nearby; she is lounging, semi-naked in a fountain, and of course, the Dublin wits nick-named her 'The Floozie in the Jacuzzi'. Not too far away there is a lovely bronze statue of Mollie Malone with her cockles and mussels cart, and of course she got the nickname of 'The Tart With the Cart'.

* * *

I feel compelled to write a few lines about the sad story of the 'Rose of Tralee'. Her name was Mary O'Connor and she was a maidservant who fell in love with a rich man in the town. He also loved her, but both families objected to the union. The lover, a certain William Pembroke Mulchinock, was broken hearted and wrote a beautiful song to win her heart. The song won her over but she would not split him from his family, so she declined his love. He emigrated to far away places but he could not get Mary out of his mind, so years later he returned to Tralee to try to rekindle the painful romance. On his way to see Mary, William decided to have a drink to give himself 'Dutch Courage'. The publican drew the blinds as a funeral procession was passing outside, and William inquired as to who the deceased was. The landlord replied, 'It's Mary O'Connor, The Rose of Tralee'. Poor old William was speechless.

A few years later William married an old flame and emigrated to New York, where they produced a couple of children. But as the years sped by he could not get Mary out of his mind, so he returned to Tralee alone, just to be near the grave of his long lost sweetheart. He died when he was in his forties and is now interred in a grave next to his beloved Mary. Would that bring a tear to one's eye or not? This happened in the 1800s, when the Great Famine in Ireland was then in progress. William's time was 1820 to 1864. I feel compelled to write the first verse from that most beautiful poetic song, 'The Rose of Tralee':

The pale moon was rising above the green mountains,
The sun was declining beneath the blue sea,
When I strayed with my love by the pure crystal fountain
That stands in the beautiful vale of Tralee.

Just think of those beautiful words that paint a most vivid and colourful picture in the mind. You do not need a brush or paint to create this scene.

Chapter 43

I must now return from my nostalgic trip to Ireland and tell you about my first TV job in the post office sorting depot in Rathbone Place, just off Oxford Street. I was taken by lift deep under ground to service a TV that never had any chance of getting a picture – this was due to the fact that there was no aerial this deep down in the bowels of the building. Anyway, as I was waiting for the lift to arrive so that I could return to the surface, I heard a loud sound coming from a large hole in the wall. It was a miniature electric train complete with carriages emerging from that very opening. I asked my escort, 'What the hell is that?'

He told me that it was the Royal Mail underground train. He said that it runs from Paddington to Whitechapel. It's just like a tube train only there are no passengers, and it's totally driverless. After a short while of automatic unloading, off it went on its way down the narrow-gauge track and into another hole in the opposite wall. I was mesmerised. Very few people know anything of this hidden treasure. The train was installed in 1927, and closed in 2003. By closing this bit of brilliant British engineering, lorries then had to be used to deliver the mail to and from the three giant sorting depots, thus causing even more traffic congestion. How daft was that! The train is still there but it has been mothballed.

* * *

In Bloomsbury there is the University College London, UCL for short. Here, one can find the embalmed remains of Jeremy Bentham, a philosopher who was one of the founders of UCL.

This chap has been placed in a large, highly varnished wooden case. He is sitting on one of his own armchairs and wearing his own period style attire: notice the spectacles, they definitely were not from Specsavers, also note the ring. He is dressed in his own, personally selected clothing. This case is on wheels, and I am informed that the display is rolled out to preside over the college's annual meetings.

Rumour has it that his ghost walks the corridors of this old building at night. 'How does he get out of the locked case?' you might wonder. There is another story going around that his head is not the original. It may be wax. They say that some of the student chaps stole the head and played football with it. They should have been brought before the 'Head' for punishment. I believe there may have been a joke in there somewhere. I went along to the college in order to take a photo for this book. The security people had locked the display as there was a student march that day, but these good officers actually opened the protective door and let me take my photo. It was a wee bit scary watching the door slowly open, and there he was. I must admit I was a little apprehensive when he appeared before my very eyes. Jeremy Bentham's time was 1748 to 1832.

The smallest police station in London, 'possibly in Europe', is in Trafalgar Square. It has room for one or maybe two coppers, depending on how skinny these constables are. Inside there is a telephone, and a wall shelf on which to write up the daily notes. When the phone is lifted for an emergency, a flashing light comes on to attract nearby patrolling policemen, who would be welcome in an emergency, and they could rush to the square to assist their colleagues. There were always lots of angry political demonstrations held in this square and this unique structure has all round observation slots to make it easy to spot any trouble. I am told that there were times when a couple of prisoners were also held within this police box – what a handy holding pen. I belive that the circular police station was built in 1926, and is no longer used for its original purpose. The local council now use it as a broom cupboard. What a shame. Rumour has it that the extremely ornate glass light on top of this structure was once in a proud position on board Lord Nelson's flag ship, the *Victory*.

Did you know that there was a 'Left-Handed' shop in Soho? It closed in 2006 due to rising rents and excessive parking charges. Don't these people want any of those lovely old businesses to thrive? They are closing daily. What will we be left with? Very little, I think. This shop really did help the left-handed. In Ireland, the Gaelic for a left-handed person is a 'kithogue'. I am glad to say that the 'Left-Handed' shop has now moved to the Internet, far from the reach of high rents and greedy parking charges. I actually believe that a very large portion of these rents will end up abroad, feathering foreign nests, and in no way will that help this country. These big organisations are getting out of control.

* * *

I was on the cab rank at Clapham Junction some time ago. I had not had, as they say in the cab trade, 'a wrong un' for some time, and there he was standing at my window. He looked like Albert Steptoe, except that he was well-dressed, and spoke fairly posh English.

'Can you take me to Sutton, cabbie?' he said to me.

'Jump in,' said I, and off we went.

When we arrived in Sutton I asked him where exactly it was that he wanted. He said, 'It doesn't look very much like Sutton.' He then said, out of the blue, 'Can you take me to Battersea?' and named a certain pub. It was then that I realized I had a mentally ill person in the cab. I had to get back to London, so he may as well come with me, I just could not leave this poor old chap in Sutton. When we got to the pub we both entered, and the moment the landlady saw us, and my badge, she shook her head. I asked her, 'What can I do?' She said that I should take him to the police station. She knew all about this guy, and she also knew that he had no money. I could not leave this elderly man on the streets of London, so I took him to the local cop shop and handed him over. They asked me if I wanted him charged for fraud, I said, 'You must be joking'. The police thanked me for my good attitude. So I left this poor old gent in their care. Even though I had been swindled I could not help feeling sorry for this senior citizen, who made me think, 'But for the grace of God, there go I'. Four hours had elapsed and I did not even earn a penny. As Frank Sinatra said, 'That's Life'.

Two officers from that very same police station were in attendance a couple of years earlier when a car driver turned left and crashed into my cab. Regardless of the fact that there was a 'No Left Turn' sign, the cops said, 'Sort it out between yourselves,' and walked away. All I could do was take the car's number plate, which was false, and the driver's address. That turned out to be a cemetery in Tooting (but which grave? Ha,ha.) When I complained about the policemen's behaviour, all I got was an apology. I suppose if I had got myself a good lawyer I may have received compensation. But there you have it.

In my twenty-seven years as a black cab driver, the odd fiddling punter has got into my cab, and when we get to the train or coach station they say that they have been robbed, or lost their wallet or purse. I have heard that story time after time. So what can I do? I give my address, and they say they will send the fare. In twenty-seven years, not one has ever sent me the fare that they owed me. I hear complaints about cabbies from the public, but it's equal on both sides: ninety-nine per cent of punters and cabbies are honest. By the way, it's the Lord Mayor's 'Transport for London' who set the taxi tariffs, not the cabbie. Also the meter is offically sealed and cannot be tampered with.

* * *

I was passing Wandsworth Prison one morning around 9am, when I was hailed by a newly released prisoner. He looked OK so I stopped and picked him up. This guy was glad to be out, and I was sure that he would not do anything that would put him straight back in the clink, so I felt safe. We started chatting, and he told me that he had been sentenced to twelve years for murder, ten of which was in the Isle of Wight's Parkhurst prison, and the remaining two years in Wandsworth Prison. He also told me that his toughest time was the two years in Wandsworth. But, if you were a model prisoner in Wandsworth you could get anything sent in: fags, whisky, drugs, all sorts of stuff. He said, 'It depends on who you know'. I am unable to substantiate any of this information as I don't even know this fellow's name. This ex-con told me that he went to the aid of his mother who was being abused by her live-in lover. He said that he had lost his temper, and stabbed the lover to death in order to protect his mum. I actually felt sorry for this poor fellow. It's a natural action to protect one's mother, but the judge did not think that way. I took him to the nearest public house so that he could drink to his welcome release. His mother was still alive, and he said that he was longing to see her, but the pint of ale was all that was on his mind.

I once picked up a man outside Battersea power station. He was a senior engineer in this unique building. He casually related to me that this was the largest single brick building in Europe. He further told me that the excess hot water was piped under the Thames to provide central heating for the council houses and blocks of flats in Churchill Gardens, Pimlico. What a great bit of engineering, otherwise the hot water would have been wastefully pumped into the river. I suppose it would have kept the fish warm. I am sure that all the heating bills went up when the power station closed in 1983. Battersea power station was built in the 'Art Deco' style and looks just like a giant upside-down table to me. The power station will soon be redeveloped, possibly by the Japanese, who I believe have futuristic plans for this slowly decaying structure. The building was used in the Monty Python film *The Meaning of Life* and has also appeared in *Doctor Who*, and many other films whose titles elude me.

Speaking of council houses, a housing councillor asked an Eskimo, 'What do you think of the housing shortage?' to which he replied, 'I have not got igloo'. He may have mispronounced 'a clue'. It's only a weak joke.

* * *

I went on a last trip to central London in order to take a few more photos for this book. I was in Whitehall and I have never seen so many tourists, all taking photos of the splendidly attired troopers on horseback. A few took a picture of the three hundred-year-old clock behind the Guards, but they failed to notice a large black spot just at the top of the two o'clock numeral on this timepiece. This black spot denotes the exact time that the executioner's axe struck the neck of King Charles I, severing the head from his body with one clean blow. I have often wondered if the victim can actually see the basket as his head crashes into the container. Surely there must be micro-seconds before the brain shuts down, and during this tiny amount of time this image is passed to the brain, and must show pure terror to the beholder. I read somewhere that the eyes of the severed head of the French Queen, Marie Antoinette, were open when it entered the basket, and these terror filled eyes rolled in their sockets for around ten to fifteen seconds. How horrible is that? Man has always been cruel to his fellow man, and this will never change.

I strolled up to the Houses of Parliament and took an awesome picture of the fierce-looking Oliver Cromwell's statue. Cromwell was supposed to have said to a portrait painter that he wanted a correct likeness of himself, 'warts and all'. They say that this is where that saying comes from, but there is no real evidence of this story, but it does sound plausible. I must admit that the image looks very foreboding. I would not like to meet this man in a battle, look at the size of his sword. I'm afraid that I would have to take to my heels.

I then walked past the original Jewel House. They actually kept the Crown Jewels here for well over 300 years. In 1671, a Colonel Thomas Blood did actually steal the jewels, was caught, sentenced to death, and later reprieved by King Charles II. So the treasures were moved to the impregnable, and ever so fearsome Tower of London, where they have been safe ever since. If one looks at the photo of the old Jewel House, it does not look very secure. I certainly wouldn't keep 'my' jewels there, such as they are.

In Piccadilly (Knightsbridge end), there is a strange object called the Porter's Rest. Around the late 1700s the porters from Covent Garden would be carrying in excess of a dozen loaded baskets on their heads. So the local do-gooders erected what looked like a giant, long bench seat so that the porter could rest without putting his load on the ground. He would never be able to lift the baskets from the ground back on to his head, but with the bench at shoulder level, it's easier to just bend the knees, move the baskets on to the bench, rest, reload, and then continue his journey. The Porter's Rest could accommodate about ten basket loads at one time. (See photo in plate section.)

I continued my London walk, and arrived in the very upmarket Eaton Square, where I came across a blue plaque to Vivien Leigh. She was a Hollywood legend in the old films such as *Gone With The Wind* with Clark Gable, *A Streetcar Named Desire*, *Waterloo Bridge*, and so on.

As I was walking down Whitehall, I could not resist taking a photo of a couple of rare red phone boxes. I wonder how much longer they will be there.

* * *

I am now heading for one of the world's most famous department stores, Harrods. This store is actually in Brompton Road, and not in the street called Knightsbridge, but it is in the area affectionately known as Knightsbridge. There was a time when this store had a strict dress code, no soldiers in uniform, no flipflops or bare midriffs, and definitely no shorts. Today, the rules are a bit more lenient, but it still has the no shorts policy.

Henry Harrod started his business with a small shop on the site. He was a tea merchant, and soon expanded the store to be the largest department store in Europe. I was informed that in the early years the store could take you from the cradle to the grave, they would even supply the coffin, plus the service. Harrods employs up to 4,000 workers. The food hall would knock one down with its fabulous aromas making one's mouth water. Some people who cannot afford to shop in this high-class store just buy the famous green carrier bag, shop elsewhere, then they go home swinging the full-up, prestigious bag so all the neighbours can see. That sounds like the 'fur coat and no drawers' theme.

This fine store has been there since 1884, and boasts the very first escalator. A cuddly toy bear was purchased by a certain A A Milne for his son who was called Christopher Robin. He named the bear 'Winnie the Pooh', and then came the famous Winnie the Pooh stories. Harrods is worth a visit even if it's only for the green carrier bag.

Just around the corner from Harrods is Hans Place. Here at number 23 there is a blue plaque dedicated to the novelist Jane Austen. She lived there in the year 1814. This talented lady wrote *Pride and Prejudice* and *Sense and Sensibility* among many others. If we walk further along Brompton Road we come across Beauchamp Place (pronounced Beecham Place). It is well over 200 years old, and is one of the most fashionable places in London. People from Princess Diana to Kirk Douglas have been seen here. In the early 1800s an upper-crust shopper would have an armed escort to protect them from 'footpads, ruffians and murderers'. But nothing changes, the low life still turns up now and then. A poor old jeweller closed up after being robbed three or four times. He was there for years, and then he said that he had had enough. He feared that the next time he may be shot dead.

* * *

I was surprised when I read an article about one of the largest meat markets in Europe, Smithfield. The article said that during the plague this area was a large open field. As the plague deaths were mounting, they buried over 50,000 victims here; what an enormous number of expired human beings to bury, presumably in mass graves. Also on this site up to 300 people were burnt at the stake in religious persecutions. What a bloodthirsty place this was in days of yore.

The market is a great place to visit today. Just before Christmas is the best time to experience the exciting hustle and bustle. Do you think that if the people of this meat market dug down deep enough they would find bones? And would the plague virus still be active? Incidentally, the porters of this meat market are called 'bummarees'. What a strange name.

Chapter 44

Going back about twenty years, I remember being on the rank at Paddington Station, third cab in line, when two Americans ladies came to my window and asked to be taken to the London Palladium. I said there were two cabs in front of me, to which they replied, 'But one is red and the other is blue and yours is black'. They went on to say, 'We were told to only use black cabs in London'.

By this time the two taxis in front were gone, so the Yanks got into my vehicle. I explained that the term 'black cab' is an affectionate term that refers to all licensed taxis, no matter what colour. These ladies had been in London for about a week and had missed out time and again by waiting for a 'black taxi' while they watched lots of coloured cabs drive by without hailing them.

As we pulled out of the station, all traffic came to a sudden standstill. Apparently, a terrorist was priming a bomb in a top floor bedsit in Sussex Gardens. The device blew up in his face. I read later in the evening news that the bomber was deeply imbedded in the ceiling plaster and the police forensic team literally had to climb a stepladder and scrape off what was left of him. The good thing was that no other person was killed. The bad thing was that my two Americans got out and walked to the Palladium, so I lost the fare.

Another time in the same station I picked up a Chinese tourist. He said in broken English that he wanted to go to the Windsor Castle. I said to this Oriental gent, 'I am very sorry, but it's only ten a.m. and the pubs do not open until eleven'. He said, 'Nooo, I no wan dink, I wan see wer king n' queen liv, you take now, prease, Windsor Castle.' That's exactly how he spoke. What a great fare, all the way to the real Windsor Castle, but it's a good thing that I mentioned the opening hours or he would have looked at the pub and said, 'No very big castle, wer queen?' As we drove away from the station I could not help thinking that this was my first Chinese takeaway of the week...

* * *

I was hailed in the Edgware Road once by five Middle Eastern ladies. Four of them were extremely petite in stature. The fifth was much larger and I thought she was the matriarch of the group because she held the purse and was the only one to speak. They all wore jet black burkas and were covered in black fabric from head to toe. I looked in the rear view mirror and all I could see was the whites of their stunning eyes in a background of darkness. It was a most unusual sight. I had the feeling I was driving around a small part of some lucky man's harem. They asked to be driven to Berkeley Square. When we arrived at Berkeley Square, the large lady said, 'We have come to hear the nightingales'. Well, I was well and truly flabbergasted. I explained that it was only a line from the Frank Sinatra song, 'A Nightingale Sang in Berkeley Square.'

She thought for a few seconds, and then uttered 'Oh', and without hesitation said, 'Take us to Shepherd's Bush market'. I couldn't help laughing with my mouth shut.

* * *

As a television engineer in the sixties I was once called to Down Street, just off Piccadilly. As far as I could make out, the flat was rented by Jackie Kennedy's sister-in-law, and the First Lady was there. Apparently it was a clandestine visit about some family affairs and the press did not even know she was in London. I suppose I could have made a fortune if I had phoned the newspapers.

I actually caught a brief glimpse of the First Lady of America when she threw a tiny, brief smile at me before disappearing into another room. I still treasure that little smile. She had her bodyguard close by her side and I was surprised that I was even let into the mansion flat without a proper security check.

When one of the greatest American presidents of our time was shot dead, Jackie waited out the proper mourning period and then married the shipping magnate Aristotle Onassis in 1968. I wanted to draw a cartoon of this lovely lady depicting her walking in a field full of donkeys, and the caption would have read 'At last Jackie has got her "own asses"'. I do hope that I don't have to explain that joke. I am a terrible cartoonist, so it never materialised.

Chapter 45

I was on the Harrods cab rank and while there was a lull in trade I began thinking back to a few years before when there was a terrible accident on this very spot. Two American tourists were window-shopping when suddenly a black cab came around the corner. The driver's foot had got stuck between the brake and the accelerator and the taxi mounted the pavement and drove straight over the two unfortunates, killing them instantly. The vehicle ended up in Harrods' window. I was told the driver was wearing sandals that may have been too big for him and the wide sole had got jammed between the accelerator pedal and the brake pedal. Imagine, coming all the way from America, just to get killed.

Suddenly, I was brought back down to earth by a tap on the window. It was a stunningly dressed lady wearing sunglasses. Before she could speak, I said 'number "xxx" Eaton Place'. (I cannot reveal the number of this nice female's flat in order to protect her privacy.) She then said, 'How did you know that?' to which I replied, 'You are Joan Collins, are you not?' She dropped her sunglasses a little, and said, 'Yes I am'. She was slightly miffed that I had recognised her.

I drove Miss Collins to her London home with very little conversation but I did tell her that the famous Vincent Price (1911–1993) once lived opposite her, and that I was his television engineer at one time. I remember I was quite anxious as I rang the Price household bell, hoping he was not home as I had recently watched one of his scary movies called *House of Wax*. But in fact I was delighted when he came to the door with a big smile. After all, he was only acting in all those scary films and when I met him he was a lamb, and married to the actress Coral Brown.

* * *

In 1981, just before the Falklands war, I paid regular television visits to a Naval commander. I think he was an Argentine Naval Attaché to this country. I became quite friendly with this man, his wife and their beautiful young daughter. I don't know why he befriended me, I could hardly understand what he was saying and I certainly could not pronounce his long name. He sent a few presents to my family, and I never left his Sloane Street flat without an expensive bottle of Napoleon brandy.

After six months had elapsed, he and his family were suddenly recalled to Argentina, which must have had something to do with the surprise attack on the Falkland Islands. I later spoke to the doorman of the flats in question, who said the family had departed in a hurry. The day before they left, our Navy man told the porter that Denis Thatcher had acquired shares in oil fields just off the coast of the Falkland Islands. It makes one wonder, was there something going on behind the scenes? Did we go to war to protect the islanders or was it to protect the oil? I have often wondered about that Naval commander customer of mine, was he ever on the Belgrano and did he survive that awful war, or did he just do a runner?

* * *

Before I finish my little tale, I have to admit that I was once overtaken by a four-poster bed on the motorway, complete with blankets, sheets, and pillows. The 'vehicle' had four wheels, an engine, lights, number plates and was fully licensed to be on the road. (See photo in plate section.)

The bed was doing sixty mph and it's a bit embarrassing to admit that it was going faster than my brand new taxi. I assume the bed was on its way to Bedfordshire...

* * *

I now spend my evenings singing and dancing in an extremely friendly working man's premises in south west London called the Tooting Progressive Club. This club is very proud of its unique juke box that contains over 3,000 song titles, a great pool table, and brilliantly friendly staff.

I also spend an equal amount of time next door in a highly entertaining and, may I say, non 'plastic' Irish pub called The Ramble Inn in Tooting. What a watering hole! This inn entertains with open mic nights, poker nights, quiz nights and on a Sunday night one can hear fantastic traditional live Irish music. Of course, spontaneous singing is any night. The bar staff are quite unique, especially Eamon, the world's greatest barman.

I love doing nothing now and there's so much nothing to be done that I have no time on my hands at all!

* * *

Remembering all the famous names and places, the incidents and accidents, the ordinary and the extraordinary, over fifty-five years of working in London, is a pretty big task for anyone. In this book I hope I have recalled most of the more exciting parts of my life, both as a cabbie and as a television engineer. Re-creating my mythical cab journey around London where I revisited those memories, I realised just how interesting my working life had been. After all, how many people can say that they have met Tom Jones, John Mills, Barry Gibb and Joan Collins, to say nothing of all the other famous people who crossed my path? Be lucky, as they say in the cab trade. I know I have been.

I ... ngie Smith for
her ... Without her, it
may ... e also involved
in ...